S

THE
BUSINESS SCHOOL
IN THE 1980s

THE

BUSINESS SCHOOL

IN THE 1980s

Liberalism
versus
Vocationalism

Paul S. Hugstad

PRAEGER

PRAEGER SPECIAL STUDIES • PRAEGER SCIENTIFIC

Library of Congress Cataloging in Publication Data

Hugstad, Paul S.
   The Business School in the 1980s

   Bibliography: p.
   Includes index
   1. Business education--United States. I Title.
HF1131.H83   1983   650'.07'1173   82-16601
ISBN 0-03-060586-5

Published in 1983 by Praeger Publishers
CBS Educational and Professional Publishing
a Division of CBS Inc.
521 Fifth Avenue, New York, New York 10175 U.S.A.

© 1983 by Praeger Publishers

3456789   052   987654321

Printed in the United States of America

To Alfred John Hugstad,

without whom my personal choices between the
liberal and the useful would not have been possible

CONTENTS

LIST OF TABLES AND FIGURES

PREFACE

A topic presently of great interest and concern on university campuses is the relative surge in business school enrollments and the accompanying decline of enrollments in liberal arts.

Present-day career pressures toward greater and greater curriculum specialization have met with mixed reactions not only across campuses but in the business community as well. Not since the days of the Foundation Reports has the discussion concerning the useful versus the liberal received such emphasis. Discussions concerning the appropriate role of the business school of the 1980s are further complicated by shrinking financial support for higher education and the changing demographics of both education and job markets.

Having recently observed the 100-year anniversary of the business school—and with the pendulum of history presently swinging back toward vocationalism in higher education—it is time to once again examine the appropriate relationship of the business school to both the university and the business community it serves. To this end, this volume examines the views of a nationally stratified sample of deans of business schools and deans of liberal arts colleges and compares them with those of university and corporate personnel directors regarding the appropriate role of business education. In order to provide a context within which these views can best be understood, this volume also presents a historical perspective on the evolution of the business school and its relationship to the liberal arts. Finally, based on the above, a set of recommendations aimed at dealing with a number of problems currently confronting business schools is offered.

For those interested in a more exhaustive examination of some of the issues dealt with in this study, a detailed bibliography is appended.

ACKNOWLEDGMENTS

This book is the result of a continuing personal interest for more than two decades in the appropriate role of business education. Beginning with my personal introduction to the worth and importance of liberal education as a student at St. Olaf College, and later during my graduate education at the University of Wisconsin, a number of superior professors have helped shape my views regarding the appropriate training for business careers.

Over the past decade I have had the privilege of associating with colleagues of differing persuasions at a number of universities across the country, and they have also helped shape my views on business education. To all of the above I express my thanks.

Special thanks are offered to Dr. Robert M. Barath, California State University, Fullerton, for his assistance during the design and data collection stages of the Deans Survey and for numerous insights as a colleague over the past years.

I also extend my appreciation to the School of Business Administration and Economics, California State University-Fullerton, and especially the Department of Marketing for helping support this undertaking.

Much of the financial support for completing the Deans Survey portion of this book was provided by the Shelby Cullom Davis Foundation, New York.

To Karen Murray, who worked so conscientiously and patiently typing this manuscript, I offer my sincere thanks.

Finally, to my wife, Wendelyn, and my sons, Erik and Jonathan, I offer my sincere appreciation for their patience and understanding during the writing of this book.

THE
BUSINESS SCHOOL
IN THE 1980s

1

HISTORICAL DEVELOPMENT
OF THE
BUSINESS SCHOOL

The debate over the appropriate role of business education has been going on in varied form continuously for the 100-year history of the business school. This debate is lodged in the historical roots of the business school within the liberal arts college, and is, in part, due to the changing natures of both the university and the business environment over the last century. In order to better understand the present-day debate and issues concerning the relationship of the business school to other university components and to the business community, a brief history of the evolution of the business school is in order.

FOUNDING PERIOD (1881-1900)

American business education can be traced back as far as the early nineteenth century in the form of private business colleges and trade schools teaching the basics of bookkeeping, arithmetic, and commercial law. The emphasis was primarily on training clerks, while the managerial and administrative aspects of business were largely ignored.[1] What we today know as business schools are typically dated from the establishment of the Wharton School in 1881. Business schools are uniquely American among professional schools, with their rather late origins being found in liberal education. The American value system's emphasis on free enterprise and accumulation of wealth gave the study of commerce in the United States a status not enjoyed by European countries. Even so, the business school was a late arrival upon the scene.[2]

1

The earliest period of university-based business education was shaped by men of wealth who financially contributed to universities following the Civil War. Their concern was primarily in providing a good general education to young gentlemen of wealth and privilege.[3]

The first collegiate business school, the Wharton School of Finance and Economy, was founded in 1881 at the University of Pennsylvania. Joseph Wharton's initial gift of $100,000 was to be used to educate the young men of prominent families for careers in government and business. The Wharton School remained under the umbrella of the College of Arts and Sciences until 1912 when it was given autonomy with its own dean and faculty.[4]

The early programs such as that at the Wharton School were decidedly liberal in nature. "Higher education for business thus began in considerable part as a means for educating gentlemen. It was to provide more character development than vocational training, to emphasize moral and intellectual training, but not lead directly to a career."[5]

Before the end of the century, business schools were also established at the University of California and the University of Chicago. These prototypes were quickly followed by business schools at New York University, the University of Wisconsin, the University of Michigan, and Dartmouth College's Amos Tuck School. The Harvard Business Graduate School was founded in 1908.[6]

PRAGMATIC PERIOD (1900-18)

The turn-of-the-century demands of rapidly expanding industries led to a rapid expansion of both business schools and the accompanying business literature. In the forefront of much of this growth was the pressure to professionalize the accounting function.

Much of the growth and popularity of business schools during this period was attributed to their tendency toward more and more narrowly specialized course offerings, moving away from their liberal arts underpinnings and toward the practical. Emphasis was placed on entry-level skill development rather than on long-range administrative and management skills. This pragmatic orientation, coupled with the relatively low cost of producing business school graduates (versus such schools as engineering and medicine) triggered a rapid rise in business school student enrollments.[7]

TABLE 1.1

Undergraduate Business Degrees, 1914-20

Academic Year	Total Degrees
1914/15	615
1915/16	789
1917/18	640
1919/20	1,559

Source: Adapted from James Bossard and J. Frederic Dewhurst, University Education for Business (Philadelphia: University of Pennsylvania Press, 1931), p. 255.

During this period nearly all business schools moved toward the practical; this change in emphasis in turn generated sizable growth (see Table 1.1). The business schools moved toward the profession to such a degree that it was difficult to distinguish whether faculty were teachers or businessmen. [8]

MAJOR GROWTH PERIOD (1918-40)

The tremendous growth of business schools between World War I and World War II has been attributed in large part to the "bureaucratization of American business."

In the entrepreneurs' heyday of the midnineteenth century when the characteristic form of business education was an apprenticeship in business, a collegiate business school would have been an incongruity.

With the development of the large corporation, however, and its increasing dominance in American economic life, business success was less identifiable with ownership, more with a high managerial position. It was not possible for the managerial executive, as it had been for the owning executive, to pass on his social and business position to his son by simple inheritance.[9]

Business schools were increasingly viewed as vehicles to social mobility for lower income individuals seeking to join the expanding ranks of the emerging managerial class.[10] The rise in enrollments was especially evident during the decade immediately following the end of World War I. In 1918 schools of commerce granted 610 baccalaureate degrees to men and only 25 to women. By 1928 these numbers had grown to 5,474 and 1,147, respectively. Women graduates grew from being nearly nonexistent to representing 17 percent of all commerce degrees by 1928 (see Table 1.2).

Using a different measure of popular growth, registration figures also show strong growth in commerce enrollments, increasing by 85 percent between 1920 and 1928 to a total of over 67,000 stu-

TABLE 1.2

Undergraduate Business Degrees, 1920-28

Year	Total Degrees	Women	Percent Women
1920	1,599	90	10
1922	3,562	89	11
1924	4,948	92	8
1926	5,435	91	9
1928	6,621	83	17

Source: Adapted from James Bossard and J. Frederic Dewhurst, University Education for Business (Philadelphia: University of Pennsylvania Press, 1931), p. 255.

TABLE 1.3

Commerce Student Enrollments, 1920-28

Year	Students Enrolled	Percent Men	Percent Women
1920	36,456	97	3
1922	47,454	94	6
1924	56,062	92	8
1926	62,755	91	9
1928	67,496	90	10

Source: Adapted from James Bossard and J. Frederic Dewhurst, University Education for Business (Philadelphia: University of Pennsylvania Press, 1931), p. 254.

dents (see Table 1.3). During this period, the number of institutions reporting separate enrollment statistics for commerce schools also approximately doubled from 45 to 89.[11]

One difficulty in using enrollment data to estimate growth in business administration popularity is the wide divergence in the means of classifying business students used by different universities and colleges. Some institutions classify commerce students in only their junior and/or senior years, while others include freshmen and sophomores in their statistics. These discrepancies may in large part account for the fact that while women comprised only 3 percent to 10 percent of students enrolled in commerce during the 1920s, they represented from 8 percent to 17 percent of all commerce graduates over the same period (see Tables 1.2 and 1.3). Apparently women were more heavily enrolled in colleges and universities where entrance into business programs necessitated upper-class standing.

The 1920s also witnessed attempts to broaden the functional business perspective of students in production, marketing, and fi-

TABLE 1.4

Ten Largest Business Schools in 1926
(undergraduate degrees granted)

Rank	Institution	Commerce Degrees (male)
1	New York University	678
2	University of Pennsylvania	499
3	Univeristy of Illinois	306
4	Ohio State University	184
5	University of California, Berkeley	181
6	Syracuse University	160
7	University of Washington	120
8	University of Pittsburgh	111
9	University of Nebraska	102
10	University of Minnesota	93

Source: Adapted from James Bossard and J. Frederic Dewhurst, University Education for Business (Philadelphia: University of Pennsylvania Press, 1931), p. 257.

nance and to give added emphasis to managerial consideration. These attempts were, in general, thwarted as students continued their rush into increased specialization within their various majors.

Table 1.4 lists the ten largest business schools in terms of undergraduate commerce degrees granted in 1926. The majority of these schools at that time offered considerable specialization in the various functional areas.

The introduction of the now famous Harvard case method in the early 1920s brought a vehicle for integration and vigorous reasoning to those graduate business schools with financial resources to follow. [12]

The depression atmosphere of the 1930s showed its effect on business schools, further swelling enrollments and legitimizing the professors of vocationalism. University enrollments took a notice-

TABLE 1.5

Business Degrees Earned, 1920–40

Academic Year	Degrees in Business				Master's Degrees in Business as Percentage of All Business Degrees	Business Degrees as Percentage of Degrees in All Fields	
	Bachelor's	Master's	Doctor's	All Levels		Bachelor's	All Levels
1919/20	1,576	100	0	1,676	6.5	3.2	3.2
1921/22	3,595	192	0	3,787	5.1	5.8	5.5
1923/24	5,091	267	0	5,358	5.0	6.2	5.9
1925/26	5,467	390	0	5,857	6.7	5.6	5.4
1927/28	6,748	460	3	7,211	6.4	6.1	5.8
1929/30	6,376	578	4	6,958	8.3	5.2	5.0
1931/32	9,755	1,197	35	10,987	9.4	7.1	6.8
1933/34	9,657	897	35	10,589	8.5	7.1	6.7
1935/36	9,973	698	38	10,709	6.5	7.0	6.5
1937/38	14,289	951	34	15,274	6.2	8.7	8.1
1939/40	18,549	1,139	37	19,725	5.8	10.0	9.1

Source: Robert A. Gordon and James E. Howell, Higher Education for Business (New York: Columbia University Press, 1959), p. 21.

able shift toward business schools. By 1940 business baccalaureate degrees numbered 18,549—10 percent of all degrees awarded, nearly doubling from the 5.2 percent in 1930 (see Table 1.5).[13]

In the 1930s emphasis on analytical methods began to replace the descriptive techniques of the previous period but the depression economy acted as a barrier to such change by creating a job market where functional specialization was still the preferred hiring criterion. This pressure to provide short-run marketable skills was especially heavy for large metropolitan schools.[14]

> It is hardly surprising that in the pessimistic atmosphere of the thirties many executives looked askance at any job candidate who seemingly was short on functional know-how as practiced at the lower levels of the organization. Nor is it surprising that the collegiate schools of business, particularly the large metropolitan institutions, took their cues from business and provided heavy dosages of functionalization while continuing to give lip service to ideas of producing the decision-making, management-oriented graduate.[15]

By 1940 there were 120 collegiate schools of business, of which 53 belonged to the American Assembly of Collegiate Schools of Business (AACSB). The AACSB's task was to wrestle with problems of course curriculum, academic standards, faculty credentials, and the like.[16]

POST-WORLD WAR II CHANGES

With the end of World War II came enormous growth in business school enrollments. Many new schools of business were established and most chose to pattern themselves after the older well-established schools. Enrollments in business schools peaked in 1947, and in 1950 more than 76,000 baccalaureate degrees in business were awarded (see Table 1.6). These students represented not only a quantitative change but also a qualitative change that supplied an impetus for reexamining the mission and focus of the business school. A student body comprised increasingly of older, more mature students put pressure on administrators to heighten the true educational value and long-run benefits of a business degree.[17] One

TABLE 1.6

Business Degrees Earned, 1948-58

Academic Year	Degrees in Business				Master's Degrees in Business as Percentage of All Business Degrees	Business Degrees as Percentage of Degrees in All Fields	
	Bachelor's	Master's	Doctor's	All Levels		Bachelor's	All Levels
1947/48	37,328	3,357	41	40,726	8.2	13.7	12.8
1948/49	61,624	3,897	29	65,550	5.9	16.8	15.5
1949/50	72,137	4,335	58	76,530	5.7	16.6	15.3
1950/51	58,237	4,355	65	62,657	7.0	15.2	13.7
1951/52	46,683	3,826	92	50,601	7.6	14.1	12.6
1952/53	40,706	4,035	109	44,850	9.0	13.4	12.0
1953/54	39,827	4,231	118	44,176	9.6	13.6	12.3
1954/55	40,350	4,641	144	45,135	10.3	14.0	12.7
1955/56	41,035	4,266	121	45,422	9.4	13.3	12.1
1956/57	45,455	4,575	93	50,123	9.1	13.4	12.2
1957/58	50,090	5,205	109	55,404	9.4	13.7	12.6

Source: Robert A. Gordon and James E. Howell, Higher Education for Business (New York: Columbia University Press, 1959), p. 21.

9

result of this introspection was a crystallization of the view of the business school as a rapidly evolving profession focused upon the needs of present and future executives, with a concomitant reemphasis on the social sciences as the underpinnings of a quality business education.

PERIOD OF SELF-CRITICISM AND EXAMINATION

During the late 1950s business schools underwent an unparalleled period of self-examination and criticism. Two landmark studies completed in 1959, The Education of American Businessmen and Higher Education for Business,[18] helped concentrate attention on needed changes in business school curricula, standards, and faculties. Given the wide attention gained at the time and their continuing influence on business schools of today, these studies, and the impact of their recommendations, will be examined in detail in the following chapter.

NOTES

1. Charles J. Kiernan, "The Rise of the Collegiate School of Business," in Thought Patterns: Toward a Philosophy of Business Education, ed. Blaise Opulente (New York: St. John's University Press, 1960), p. 3.

2. Earl Cheit, The Useful Arts and the Liberal Tradition (New York: McGraw-Hill, 1975), p. 83.

3. Ibid., p. 85.

4. Ibid., p. 3.

5. Ibid., p. 86.

6. Kiernan, "Rise of the Collegiate School," p. 3.

7. Cheit, The Useful Arts, p. 89.

8. Frank Pierson, The Education of American Businessmen (New York: McGraw-Hill, 1959), pp. 36-41.

9. Richard Hofstadter and Stewart Handy, The Development and Scope of Higher Education in the United States (New York: Columbia University Press, 1952), p. 90.

10. Cheit, The Useful Arts, p. 94.

11. James Bossard and J. Frederic Dewhurst, University Education for Business (Philadelphia: University of Pennsylvania Press, 1931), p. 254.

12. Kiernan, "Rise of the Collegiate School," p. 5.

13. Robert A. Gordon and James E. Howell, Higher Education for Business (New York: Columbia University Press, 1959), p. 8.

14. Kiernan, "Rise of the Collegiate School," p. 11.

15. Ibid.

16. Cheit, The Useful Arts, p. 94.

17. Gordon and Howell, Higher Education, p. 13.

18. Pierson, Education of Businessmen; and Gordon and Howell, Higher Education.

2

THE
FOUNDATION REPORTS
ERA

The period of criticism of business education reached a peak in the late 1950s with the publication of two independent, comprehensive, and highly critical Foundation studies of business schools.[1] Both Gordon and Howell (funded by the Ford Foundation) and Pierson (funded by the Carnegie Foundation) found business schools in general to be too vocational, of substandard quality regarding both students and faculty, and lacking in coherent and integrated programs at both the undergraduate and graduate levels.

FORD FOUNDATION REPORT

Gordon and Howell criticized the business school core courses for being overly descriptive and lacking in both a use of analytical techniques and a focus on managerial problem solving. The increased use of case analysis as a teaching technique was recommended to resolve this latter problem.[2] It was also documented that business education was overwhelmingly an undergraduate phenomenon. In 1957/58 approximately 20 percent of the 600 colleges and universities with degree programs in business offered master's programs, but less than 10 percent of all business degrees were master's degrees.[3]

Gordon and Howell argued strongly against this imbalance between undergraduate and graduate emphasis and against the overspecialized nature of the undergraduate business programs they examined. Their position was that at the undergraduate level a broad and general education should be offered, with courses in general education and a professional core (representing 80 percent of all units) being completed before any business electives were taken. Indeed, Gordon and Howell suggested that specialization be postponed to the graduate level, relying on work experience and training to provide much of the technical and specialized training increasingly needed by business and industry.[4]

These two researchers envisioned the M.B.A. as predominantly a two-year postbaccalaureate professional degree, and argued against too much specialization even at this level. They noted that many graduate programs were merely extensions of their own undergraduate programs, dominated by their own students. This trend was found to be especially prevalent among the large state universities. It was also noted that students in these programs were generally among the weakest of all graduate students.[5] Gordon and Howell suggested the sharp curtailment of such graduate business programs and the repositioning of the M.B.A. as a professional degree to prepare students for practicing careers, in the mode of law schools.[6]

While apprehension was expressed over the relatively modest abilities of students entering business school degree programs (especially graduate programs), even greater concern was voiced over the questionable quality of business school faculties. The rapid growth of business school enrollments over the years, coupled with the slow growth of Ph.D. programs to train business educators, had left business schools dangerously dependent on part-time and nonterminally qualified teachers.[7] Program quality was further jeopardized by university administrators' typical views of business programs as "cash cows"—low-cost popular programs that could be used to subsidize other university programs. The resulting high student/faculty teaching ratios, heavy teaching loads, and minimal support services characteristic of most business school programs resulted in many curriculum programs of dubious quality. Interestingly, these concerns—expressed over 20 years ago—as well as 1960 forecasts of increasing faculty shortages in future years largely echo the concerns of today's business school administrators.

Gordon and Howell's suggestions for improving the quality of business education can be summarized as follows:

Collegiate business education should educate for the whole career and not primarily for the first job. It should view the practice of business professionally in the sense of relating it to what we have in the way of relevant systematic bodies of knowledge. It should em-

TABLE 2.1

Professional Base or "Core" for Undergraduate Business Students

Subject	Semester Courses	Semester Units or Hours
Organization theory and management principles	2	6
The market environment and functional management	3-5	9-15
Finance		
Marketing		
Industrial relations		
Human relations		
Production or operations management		
Information and control systems	3-4	9-12
Managerial accounting		
Statistical analysis and related topics		
Advanced economics	2	6
Aggregative economics		
Managerial economics		
Legal environment of business	1	3
Integrating the management viewpoint (business policy)	1	3
Total	12-15	36-45

Source: Robert A. Gordon and James E. Howell, Higher Education for Business (New York: Columbia University Press, 1959), p. 209.

phasize the development of basic problem-solving and organizational skills and socially constructive attitudes rather than memory of facts or training in routine skills.

It should recognize that business in the decades ahead will need a higher order of analytical ability, a more sophisticated command of analytical tools, a greater degree of organizational skill, a greater capacity to deal with the external environment of business, and more of an ability to cope with rapid change than has been true in the past. [8]

Toward this end, Gordon and Howell suggested that 50 percent of a model business curriculum should comprise a strong general education based on all major areas of university coursework, 30 percent to 40 percent should be made up of high-level analytical professional core courses, and the remaining 10 percent to 20 percent could include a limited concentration (if any) of 12 semester units— of which six would be from a nonbusiness but complementary area.[9] Their suggested format for undergraduate general education and professional core curricula are presented in Tables 2.1 and 2.2.

Gordon and Howell's proposed restructuring of M.B.A. programs for students with and without undergraduate degrees in business are shown in Tables 2.3 and 2.4. It was their expressed hope that a gradual but consistent transition would be made from "Type B" programs to "Type A" programs.

TABLE 2.2

Minimum General Education Program for Undergraduate Business Students

Subject	Semester Courses	Semester Units or Hours
Humanities and fine arts	8-9	24-27
English language and literature	4-5	12-25
Humanities and fine arts electives	4	12
Natural sciences and mathematics	4-8	12-24
Mathematics	2-4	6-12
Natural sciences	2-4	6-12
Behavioral-social sciences	8	24
Behavioral sciences	2	6
Economics (elementary)	2	6
Other social sciences	4	12
Total general education component	20-25	60-75

Source: Robert A. Gordon and James E. Howell, Higher Education for Business (New York: Columbia University Press, 1959), p. 173.

TABLE 2.3

Proposed "Type A" M.B.A. Program for Students without an
Undergraduate Major in Business Administration

Subject	Approximate Semester Hours
Administration-organization-human relations	6
Economics	6-9
Managerial economics	
Aggregative economics	
Government economic policy affecting business	
Information and control	6-9
Managerial accounting	
Statistics and related topics	
Functional areas	9-12
Report writing and research	0-6
Legal, social, and political environment	6
Business policy	3-6
Total core	36-54
Specialization	0-15
Electives (including nonbusiness courses)	—

Source: Robert A. Gordon and James E. Howell, Higher Education for Business (New York: Columbia University Press, 1959),
p. 275.

The suggestion was also made that the American Assembly of
Collegiate Schools of Business (AACSB) become more active in both
setting and enforcing policy guidelines in order to upgrade standards
for accredited business schools.

CARNEGIE REPORT

Pierson's evaluation of the present state of business schools
was in close agreement with that of Gordon and Howell. Of fore-

TABLE 2.4

Proposed "Type B" M.B.A. Program for Students with and without
an Undergraduate Major in Business Administration

Subject	Approximate Semester Hours	
	Can Be Waived	Cannot Be Waived
Administration-organization- human relations	3	3-6
Economics	3	3-6
Managerial economics		
Aggregative economics		
Government economic policy af- fecting business		
Information and control	6	3-6
Accounting		
Statistics and related topics		
Functional areas	6-9	6-9
Report writing and research	0	0-6
Legal, social, and political environ- ment	0	6
Business policy	0	3-6
Total core	18-21	24-45
Specialization	0	0-15
Electives (including nonbusiness courses)	0	—

Source: Robert A. Gordon and James E. Howell, Higher Education for Business (New York: Columbia University Press, 1959), p. 277.

most concern to Pierson was the questionable quality of students enrolled in business schools.

The most acute problem exists in the four-year undergraduate schools, since only the barest handful of these institutions screen applicants or impose exacting standards for graduation. With some notable exceptions, however, this condition is found at the graduate level as well. Thus, the most important step to take in this area is to increase the number of institutions which limit their programs to students interested in, and capable of, serious academic work. [10]

Pierson also found significant fault with the curricula of business schools, suggesting that much of the current content of business education was not appropriate for university level study and should be shifted back to trade schools and community colleges. His attacks were aimed not only at the level of teaching material but also at its degree of specialization. He called for business schools to limit their specialized offerings to achieve a better balance between the liberal and the vocational.

The besetting weakness in this branch of education, as perhaps in many others is the tendency to build up areas and subareas far beyond their true academic worth. What may have once been a pioneering effort to increase the depth and scope of a field, too often turns into an elaborate departmental structure with a variety of prerequisites, course requirements, and specialized electives. A school that is genuinely interested in a managerial point of view and makes a conscientious effort to bring each of its courses within this conception of business education will necessarily limit its offerings in the various specialized areas. [11]

While Pierson agreed in general with Gordon and Howell that a better balance needed to be struck between the liberal and the vocational in business curricula, he also pointed out that given the current state of liberal education no simple transference of courses from business to liberal arts would satisfactorily accomplish this end.

The malaise of the liberal arts in American higher education has extremely complex causes but there can be no doubt that it exists on a wide scale. Therefore, any steps that are taken to shift the work of business students from the business specialties to greater emphasis on general background subjects need to be coupled with a revitalization of the liberal arts as well. Merely to require these students to take a variety of courses in nonbusiness areas taught in a perfunctory manner by instructors whose main interests lie elsewhere will not meet the situation and, in fact, do much harm.[12]

VIEWS OF BUSINESS EDUCATORS

During the 1950s (and even before the Foundation Reports), a growing number of business educators were already of the belief that business should become a profession, following the models of medicine and law. To this end, the requisite background for graduate training in business was seen as a baccalaureate in liberal arts. The rationale behind much of this shift in orientation was pointed to by Robinson:

> The specific reasons for the shift of business education to the graduate level are now familiar. As universities seek to enlarge the analytical core of professional education for business, they place greater demands on the student, and must draw on a richer background than that usually possessed by a Freshman or even a Junior. Analytically oriented programs in business are based to a great extent on the concepts and methods of other disciplines—and are, in effect, dealing with advanced work in those disciplines. Thus such business schools are virtually forced to work with graduate students, for the same reasons that graduate education in these disciplines is demanded.[13]

Such thinking led several schools of business to abandon undergraduate education entirely and to become exclusively graduate schools.

The 1950s also witnessed a debate over the most effective method of liberalizing the business curriculum. Many business professors felt that instead of requiring more units in liberal arts outside the business school, a preferable alternative was to "liberalize" business courses themselves.

We believe that behavioral sciences should not be presented as "behavioral sciences" but should be built into the subject matter area of business courses.

Business students' interests and motivation can be gravely dampened if they are exposed to materials prepared for persons whose interest is very different from their own; in addition, difficulties of vocabulary (pedantic jargon) and viewpoint can consume very large amounts of time, which could be put to far more valuable uses. [14]

In order to accomplish this liberalization, a number of business schools began to offer faculty appointments to specialists in academic disciplines such as economics, psychology, sociology, history, and law. Such appointments, in theory, would lead to a better melding of liberal and vocational curriculum needs. This trend to appoint new faculty from the social sciences, combined with the increasing popularity of business faculty trained in technical specialties within mathematics and engineering schools, led to a noticeable decline in demand for business faculty grounded primarily in business practices. This transference of influence and power from the business community to the academy, while actually begun before the Foundation Reports, clearly received added momentum from them. By the early 1960s, the popular business literature was already acknowledging this transference of leadership and power. [15]

Not all of the motivation for the changing composition of business school faculties was due to a change in ideology, however. Such changes can also be seen as a partial solution to the historic incongruity of status between the business school and other university components.

Another reason for the hiring of specialists is to be found in a desire on the part of schools of business to enhance their academic prestige. It will be recalled that schools of business have been roundly criticized for their kind of pragmatism. Much of this criticism has been directed not at the pragmatism but at the quality of the pragmatism. Every academician knows that incompetence is a much more embarrassing charge than is illiberality. On this basis it could be argued that the desire on the part of business schools to achieve academic prestige is a much more important driving force on the current scene than is the desire to turn out broadly educated and literate graduates. [16]

By the mid-1950s, evidence was already surfacing that business offerings were becoming less vocational. In a 1956 article, Wendell Taylor noted:

> In reviewing the results of the survey, there is evidence that the student is beginning to choose broadly rather than confine his studies to narrow fields. . . . Most encouraging also is the fact that the Deans express an almost universal conviction that business education offerings should be more comprehensive and less specialized. From these trends, there is real hope that the American college can be sensitive to the real needs of society and flexible enough to adopt progressive revisions to meet the challenge of change. [17]

The impact of this push to appoint more and more discipline specialists to business school faculties was succinctly summarized by Kephart, McNulty, and McGrath as early as 1963:

> Quite possibly these academicians will prove to be more favorable towards the liberal arts than their more "action-oriented" predecessors. Nevertheless, one wonders whether or not a new specialization is being substituted for an old one. Without a doubt the technical level of the training will be higher than it has been, but this is no guarantee of the education being liberal. [18]

VIEWING BUSINESS AS A PROFESSION

The evolving view of the business school as a professional school in the mold of medicine and law became increasingly viable during the 1960s. Historically the prisoner of the liberal arts, the business school had for much of its early life been shaped by liberal rather than professional viewpoints, chiefly those emanating from departments of economics.

If the liberal arts college is the grandmother, then the department of economics has served "in the dual capacity of father, and midwife" to the collegiate school of business. The attitude of the economists has constituted a second factor of primary importance in the evolution of the business curriculum, and the relation of the business school to the department of economics is one of the outstanding problems in the development of collegiate education for business. . . . To the extent that there is anything like a common or typical attitude, it may be likened to that of a petulant father who is partly proud of, partly envious of, partly skeptical of, or even antagonistic toward his offspring, who has outgrown him or is threatening to do so.[19]

The development of business schools into truly professional schools was further hampered by university politics at the highest levels. As pointed out by Bossard and Dewhurst, business schools often became political pawns to be manipulated in ways that retarded their own development.

Certain schools of business have been considered too much in the light of a good thing, financially. They have been utilized in a number of cases to make a net financial contribution to the general university budget. At places they have been exploited specifically for the benefit of the liberal arts college. At other places, they have been starved, consciously and purposively, to prevent their development as competitors to other schools and programs of the university.[20]

In summing up the early effects of such influences on the business school curriculum, Bossard and Dewhurst stated that

The commerce curricula are the product of factors other than the careful analysis and rational judgment of the commerce faculties as to the needs of their students. Desire to conciliate the arts colleges faculties, the predilections of the economists, the dominance of pioneers, and the attitude of university administrators have played their role in varying degree from school to school.[21]

However, by 1960 growing enrollments and popularity had brought a measure of self-control to business schools, which allowed sufficient autonomy to shape their own professional curricula.

As pointed out by Schiff during a symposium in honor of the fiftieth anniversary of New York University's Graduate School of Business Administration, a basic difference existed between general and professional education.

> In general education, e.g. the traditional "liberal arts" program, the ends are forever in flux and change with every major change in the values and the structure of society. But the means are amazingly stable. Subjects, courses, and curricula in general education change their labels, but rarely their contents.
>
> In professional education, by contrast, the means are always in lively ferment, with subjects, departments, courses, and methods changing continually. But the end tends to remain the same for very long periods. . . . But while business education is similar to all other professional education in its relationship between ends and means, it differs drastically from the old professions and their schools in the relationship between specialist and generalist.
>
> In all the older professions the beginner is the generalist. As the practitioner and the scholar in law and medicine advance in the profession, they become increasingly specialized. In business, however, the beginner works, of necessity, as a specialist, in one "function" or in one skill area. . . . Increasingly in business, advancement means moving from "specialist" to "generalist."[22]

Schiff goes on to point out the challenges posed for business schools in meeting the needs of four distinct constituencies: entering graduate students from science and liberal arts, entering graduate students seeking further functional specialization, specialists seeking general management training, and finally top management. Much of the confusion over what the central thrust of the business curriculum should be is directly attributable to a failure to keep these four market segments distinctly in mind.[23]

Schiff pointed to the future needs for continued professional education and for the melding of the business school into the business profession as key challenges for the future.

Above all, the challenges ahead raise serious doubt about the direction the American business school is traveling today. It is trying today to be "academically respectable," that is, to put its emphasis on "scholarly disciplines," and especially, of course, on areas that can be considered "scientific" and capable of quantification. This is undoubtedly desirable and indeed necessary. But is it enough? Or is it equally important to develop the business school as a "clinical" and as a "professional" institution, concerned with the practice of business and with the areas of uncertainty and ignorance, as well as with the areas of certainty and quantification?[24]

PROGRAM CHANGES AT TOP
BUSINESS SCHOOLS

The early 1960s saw major changes in even the well-known business schools of the day. Harvard—even though it was not a principle target of criticism in the Foundation Reports—made major curriculum changes beginning in 1963 under its new dean, George Baker. More emphasis was placed on computer-aided decision making, government's role in business, and the multinational corporation. While the case method of instruction—a hallmark of the business school since the 1920s—was retained, increasing attention was focused upon classroom lecturing in areas such as organization behavior and quantitative analysis. Second year M.B.A. students were encouraged to take up to one-half of their courses in a field of concentration (production, finance, marketing). The need for updating corporate executives on the latest management techniques led to additional emphasis on Harvard's Advanced Management Program, a refresher course for top-echelon executives.[25]

At approximately the same time, the Stanford Business School also underwent major changes under its dean, Ernest Arbuckle. Much of Stanford's curriculum emphasis was shifted from the business functional areas to economic analysis, quantitative methods, and management of human resources, along with increased emphasis on psychology and communications. Indeed, two new courses in economics and one in mathematics were added in 1961 under the specific direction of James Howell (coauthor of one of the Foundation Reports). A concerted effort was also made to maintain and improve the quality of M.B.A. program applicants through an aggressive campus recruiting program.

To ensure business school relevancy, Arbuckle set up a working advisory council of 30 prominent businessmen to advise the school on curriculum and funding matters. In addition, Stanford emphasized executive development programs and seminars as a key way of maintaining contact with the business community.[26]

The criticisms of the Foundation Reports and of business educators significantly influenced the balance between liberal and vocational in business schools over the following two decades. The 1960s witnessed a movement back toward the liberal roots of the business school and a concerted effort to correct many of the shortcomings pointed out by the reports; the 1970s would see a shift once again toward the vocational.

Chapter 3 will examine the debate between proponents of liberal and vocational education and discuss the role of the business school in the context of these two conflicting philosophies.

NOTES

1. Robert A. Gordon and James E. Howell, Higher Education for Business (New York: Columbia University Press, 1959); and Frank Pierson, The Education of American Businessmen (New York: McGraw-Hill, 1959).

2. Gordon and Howell, Higher Education, p. 189.

3. Ibid., p. 247.

4. Ibid., p. 212.

5. Ibid., p. 274.

6. Ibid., p. 248.

7. Ibid., p. 343.

8. Ibid., p. 126.

9. Ibid., p. 213.

10. Pierson, Education of Businessmen, p. ix.

11. Ibid., p. xi.

12. Ibid., p. xii.

13. William Kephart, James McNulty, and Earl McGrath, Liberal Education and Business (New York: Institute of Higher Education, Columbia University, 1963), pp. 47-48.

14. A. R. Oxenfeldt and L. Sayles, "Behavioral Sciences in the Columbia Graduate School of Business," Memorandum to Participants in Conferences on the Behavioral Sciences in Business Schools, University of Chicago, 1958.

15. Kephart, McNulty, and McGrath, Liberal Education, p. 59.

16. Ibid., p. 63.

17. Weldon Taylor, "Are Business Schools Meeting the Challenges?" Collegiate News and Views 10 (October 1956): 1-6.

18. Kephart, McNulty, and McGrath, Liberal Education, p. 72.

19. James Bossard and J. Frederic Dewhurst, University Education for Business (Philadelphia: University of Pennsylvania Press, 1931), p. 319.

20. Ibid., p. 321.

21. Ibid., p. 324.

22. Michael Schiff, "Ends and Means in Business Education," in Preparing Tomorrow's Business Leaders Today, ed. Peter Drucker (Englewood Cliffs, N.J.: Prentice-Hall, 1969), pp. 261-62.

23. Ibid., pp. 263-65.

24. Ibid., p. 287.

25. "Tailoring the Business School to New Business World," Business Week, January 19, 1963, pp. 73-76.

26. "New Look in Business Schools," Business Week, June 17, 1961, pp. 157-64.

3

LIBERALISM
VERSUS
VOCATIONALISM

The appropriate role of business education has been a source of debate for the entire 100-year history of the business school, a debate rooted in the basic historical evolution of the business school from liberal arts stepchild to its present-day status as one of the largest and most popular majors on college campuses. The discussion has, at various times, focused not only on the degree of practical orientation of business school course offerings but also on their level of rigor, teaching techniques, integration with other disciplines, and general purpose.

DEBATE WITHIN THE ACADEMY

As Cheit pointed out previously, the debate over the role of the useful versus the liberal has been waged over the centuries. [1] Aristotle's questioning of the role of education phrased over 20 centuries ago remains timeless:

> Should the useful in life, or should virtue, or should the higher knowledge be the aim of our training? All three opinions have been entertained. No one knows on what principle we should proceed. [2]

The dialogue, having begun early, heated up around the turn of the century. Thorstein Veblen, one of the harshest critics of the business school, made his feelings well known in The Higher Learning in America. He left no doubt about his dislike of the emergence of business on campus.

> The primacy among pragmatic interests has passed from religion to business, and the school of commerce is the exponent of this primacy. It is the perfect flower of the secularization of the universities.
> The professional knowledge and skill of physicians, surgeons, dentists, pharmacists, agriculturists, engineers of all kinds, perhaps even of journalists, is of some use to the community at large, at the same time that it may be profitable to the bearers of it. . . . But such is not the case with the training designed to give proficiency in business. No gain comes to the community at large from increasing the business proficiency of any number of its young men. There are already much too many of these businessmen, much too astute and proficient in their calling, for the common good. A higher average business efficiency simply raises activity and avidity in business to a higher average pitch and fervour, with very little other material result than a redistribution of ownership; since business is occupied with the competitive acquisition of wealth, not with its production. . . . The work of the College of Commerce, accordingly, is a peculiarly futile line of endeavor for any public institution, in that it serves neither the intellectual advancement nor the material welfare of the community. [3]

In direct contrast to Veblen, Cheit offers Whitehead's view of business education as a logical addition to the university in light of both the evolution of management skills and precedents set by other professional disciplines. [4]

> The conduct of business now required intellectual imagination of the same type as that which in former times had mainly passed into those other occupations (law, clergy, medicine, and science). . . . The justification for a university is that it preserves the connection between knowledge and the zest for life . . . (and) in the modern complex social organism, the adventure of life cannot be disjoined from intellectual adventure.

We need not flinch from the assertion that the main
function of such a school is to produce men with a
greater zest for business. It is a libel on human nature
to conceive that zest for life is the product of pedestrian
purposes directed toward the narrow routine of material
comforts. [5]

As noted by Kephart, McNulty, and McGrath, the evolution of
the business school toward increased specialization must be understood in the historical context of the development of higher education.

In many ways the history of higher education is the history of specialized education. Starting with a classics-
oriented liberal arts program, collegiate education has
grown in the direction of specialized training in medicine,
law, engineering, et cetera. [6]

Bossard and Dewhurst note that the proper educational role of
business education was complicated by its early development inside
the context of the liberal arts school.

Business curricula are descendants of that imperious
dowager of academic life—the liberal arts college . . .
and perhaps no factor has been so persistently important
in shaping the curricula of the collegiate schools of business as well as in other phases of their development. [7]

The demands such a childhood placed on business education were
pointed out by Kephart, McNulty, and McGrath:

Business education, however, was not originally conceived of as professional training. Business schools
were therefore forced to provide not only functional
training such as that of medicine and law, but were required to provide a general education as extensive as
that offered by the liberal arts college. [8]

The debate between liberalism and vocationalism was further complicated by the recognition that no easy dichotomy existed between liberal education and specialized training.

> We forget that it is possible to become liberally educated by the teaching and study of professional or specialized subjects in a liberal manner. . . .
> While in general I would support the proposition that there are some things which every liberally educated man should know, I fear that we have been led into error sometimes by believing that the study of certain subject matter inevitably results in a liberal education. This is a doubtful proposition. It is nearer to the truth to say that there is no subject matter, worthy of a place in the curriculum of a modern Land-Grant College or state university, which cannot be taught either as a professional specialty or as liberal subject. [9]

Support for the liberal approach applied to the study of business was offered by a former dean of the Fordham Business School.

> Not only can it (business administration) be taught liberally but it is clamoring to be taught liberally. It has more to teach better worth knowing—in my judgment—than much of Horace and Sappho, Thackeray and Faulkner, or Edna St. Vincent Millay. Business occupies more of the average man's life than does politics, for example, and it has an influence upon human society as deep and as steady as politics. It is, therefore, as worthy of careful, scientific, social study as politics. Political science is already a respectable field of learning; business deserves to become one. [10]

In the view of John Clarke, it is more a question of when—not whether—specialized business training is provided.

> The dilemma of business education is the dilemma of the modern industrial society; that is, a culture split into three groups: scientists, businessmen, and the liberally educated. Each group is incomplete, intellectually and practically, without the other. The scientist who

can read only his own textbook is at best a one-eyed
man. The overspecialized business student is equally
purblind. But the arts student without a knowledge of
business activities, their scope and complexity, cannot
claim to be well educated. In business education, the
strongest case is not for the elimination of specialist
training as such but for learning more widely for a
longer time before the student is allowed to follow his
bent. [11]

The debate over the relative importance of general versus
specific business educational orientation was well discussed during
the self-examination period of the late 1950s. The authors of
Thought Patterns pointed to the dilemma posed by the choice between liberalism and vocationalism.

Few eternal verities exist to guide us in the solution of
the problem (generalism vs. specialism). The proper
curriculum mix is not one that can be solved for all time.
The end formation must always compromise the desired
degree of broadness and depth, ideally conceived, and
the minimum educational level required for entrance to
the business community. The latter, incidentally, will
vary from time to time with the growth of specialized
knowledge and the evolving role of business in society.
Society may call for more functionalized education in one
era and, at another point of time, require a higher level
of general education and synthesization to accomplish its
purpose. We are now passing through a period where the
stress is less on specialization and more on integration. [12]

In their analysis of the issues, Gordon and Howell suggested a
rationale for keeping the study of business decidedly liberal.

All this suggests something about the kinds of knowledge
and abilities required of the businessman. To cope with
a continuously changing nonmarket environment, he needs
breadth of knowledge, a sense of historical perspective,
and flexibility of mind. He needs also to have a sensitive
and sophisticated appreciation of the role which business
does and can play in our kind of society. All this implies

some familiarity with the more relevant branches of history and perhaps philosophy, and some knowledge of the social sciences, particularly economics, political science, and sociology. Implied also is some appreciation of the nature and significance of scientific and technological developments. The acquisition of knowledge in these different areas ought to bring a sense of historical perspective, contribute to flexibility of mind, and help to develop a sense of responsibility to the larger society of which the businessman is a part. [13]

The authors of Thought Patterns, however, rejected Gordon and Howell's generalistic prescriptions.

We feel the Ford Foundation authors misread the issues involved. "The crux of the debate was never concentration per se but the degree and quality of specialization." If business colleges have a raison d'être at all, it is to prepare the student for his first employment in one of the functional areas as well as to instill the virtues and attributes necessary for advanced professional assignments. A generalized exposure to business subjects will not suffice to accomplish the objective of collegiate education for business.

Moreover, the pattern of higher education in America, especially in the liberal arts and sciences, allows a degree of specialization far beyond the modest limits now prescribed in business curricula. To pursue a rigorous course of study in finances, accounting, marketing, and so forth, is no more liberal or vocational than to garner 30 or more credits above the introductory courses in English literature or American history. [14]

They summarized their views on the subject as follows:

A correct appreciation of the role of business education in today's business and social environment calls for a twofold integration: it must relate the specialized business subjects of accounting, marketing, or finance to certain of the underlying disciplines found in the sciences and humanities; and it must also relate these functional business subjects in their particular contributions to the decision-making process. Avoiding the extremes of specialism and generalism, education for modern business demands curricula with a balanced fusion of theory and fact, of analysis and description. [15]

In summary, the debate over liberal versus useful entailed questions of not only breadth versus depth of subject matter covered —and the level of rigor of the material taught—but also a discussion on the very meaning of the word "liberal." The challenge held out to business education, then, was not only one of balancing these orientations but also one of effectively integrating the liberal and useful in the business curriculum and across campus. Ironically, such a challenge has seldom been attempted, let alone met, within the liberal arts school itself.

VIEW FROM THE BUSINESS COMMUNITY

In the past, the views of business executives have generally suggested a strong need for a liberal arts background as a prerequisite for successful business leadership. Quoting the then president of Yale and Toune Manufacturing Company:

The qualifications needed for leadership in industry are developed largely through a liberal arts education. Let us stop for a moment and repeat what is perhaps obvious. The phrase "the liberal arts" means the arts appropriate to a free man. These arts originally were seven: grammar, rhetoric, logic, music, arithmetic, geometry, and astronomy. The purpose of these studies was not to fill the human mind with facts; it was to train the student to use his mind, to have intellectual curiosity, taste, moral strength, and imagination. The scope of liberal arts has been broadened to include many other disciplines, among them literature, languages, and fine arts. For most students, none of these has a specific vocational value, but all of them contribute to the enrichment of intellect and judgment. This enrichment is not produced by superspecialized training. [16]

However, as William H. Whyte, Jr., pointed out over 25 years ago in The Organization Man, what businessmen say and what they do are often divergent.

> This brings us to an interesting anomaly. Lately, leaders of U.S. business have been complaining that there are nowhere near enough "generalists." The average management man, they have been declaring, has been far too narrowly educated. . . . Give us the well-rounded man, business leaders are saying to the colleges, the man steeped in fundamentals; we will give him the specialized knowledge he needs.
> Convention after convention they make this plea—and their recruiters go right on doing what they've been doing: demanding more specialists. This does not spring from bad faith. The top man may be perfectly sincere in asking for the man with a broad view—he might even be a liberal arts man himself. Somewhere along the line, however, this gets translated and retranslated by the organization people, so that by the time the company gets down to cases the specifications for its officer candidates are something quite different. [17]

Pinning down business executives as to what, exactly, they want in the form of business education and determining the degree of convergence of their views with those of personnel directors were two of the principle recommendations made by Kephart, McNulty, and McGrath in their 1963 study of business education. [18]

Whyte added yet another wrinkle to the problem of correctly uncovering the true meaning of executives' views.

> It is a plausible hypothesis that many of the people who have spoken in favor of what they call liberal education are in the last analysis partisans of changes in business training which are quite clearly illiberal in the essential components. To demand training in how to get along with people, or in public speaking, is to demand something other than liberal education, no matter what department of a university happens to be in charge of the course or what the course is called. [19]

It was in part to shed some light on these conflicting views concerning the relative desirability and balance of a liberal arts versus vocational education that a study of deans and personnel directors was undertaken. The question regarding the congruence of attitudes within the business organization (between executives and personnel functionaries) is presently being treated in a parallel but separate study.

In the final analysis, the debate over the definitions, appropriate balance, and relative merits of a liberal versus vocational education can be reduced in large measure to basic value discrepancies among role occupants. These discrepancies exist in part because of differential socialization processes and in part are likely explained by role justification mechanisms.

The magnitude of differences in values and attitudes between deans of liberal arts, deans of business schools, university placement directors, and corporate personnel directors are empirically examined in Chapter 5.

NOTES

1. Earl Cheit, The Useful Arts and the Liberal Tradition (New York: McGraw-Hill, 1975), p. 3.

2. Aristotle, Politics, trans. Benjamin Jowett, bk. 8, sec. 2, 1095, p. 301.

3. Thorstein Veblen, The Higher Learning in America (New York: B. W. Huebesch, 1918), p. 205.

4. Cheit, The Useful Arts, pp. 11, 87.

5. Alfred North Whitehead, The Aims of Education and Other Essays (New York: Macmillan, 1967), pp. 94-95.

6. William Kephart, James McNulty, and Earl McGrath, Liberal Education and Business (New York: Institute of Higher Education, Columbia University, 1963), p. 32.

7. James Bossard and J. Frederic Dewhurst, University Education for Business (Philadelphia: University of Pennsylvania Press, 1935), pp. 317-18.

8. Kephart, McNulty, and McGrath, Liberal Education, p. 32.

9. Vergil N. Hancher, "Liberal Education in Professional Curricula," Proceedings of the 67th Convention of the American Association of Land Grant Colleges and State Universities 67 (1953): 45.

10. Michael McPhelin, "The Humanities and Education for Business," Collegiate News and Views 8 (October 1954): 3.

11. John Clark, "An Integrated Program for Business Education," in Thought Patterns: Toward a Philosophy of Business Education, ed. Blaise Opulente (New York: St. John's University Press, 1960), p. 74.

12. John Clark and Blaise Opulente, "Business and Liberal Arts," in Thought Patterns, ed. Blaise Opulente (New York: St. John's University Press, 1962), p. 28.

13. Robert A. Gordon and James E. Howell, Higher Education for Business (New York: Columbia University Press, 1959), p. 65.

14. Clark and Opulente, "Business and Liberal Arts," p. 28.

15. Ibid.

16. Robert A. Goldwin and Charles A. Nelson, "Specific Needs for Leadership in Management," in Toward the Liberally Educated Executive (New York: Fund for Adult Education, 1959), pp. 3-4.

17. William H. Whyte, Jr., The Organization Man (Garden City, N.Y.: Doubleday, 1956), p. 101.

18. Kephart, McNulty, and McGrath, Liberal Education, p. 74.

19. William H. Whyte, Jr., "The New Illiteracy," Saturday Review, November 21, 1953, p. 35.

4

THE RISE
OF THE
NEW VOCATIONALISM

A BRIEF MOVEMENT TOWARD THE ACADEMY

The decade of the 1960s saw the movement of the business
school temporarily away from the profession toward the academy.
Much of this shift in orientation can be traced directly to the criticism of the Foundation Reports, but it must also be credited in part
to the more liberal attitudes developing on most campuses during
the first full-scale assault of the baby-boom generation. Enrollments grew not only in business schools but in nearly all sectors of
the university, consequently removing most disciplines from the
pressures of "labor market relevance." It was during this period
that business schools solidified their core programs and added considerable rigor from the behavioral sciences and mathematics in the
process.

Many of the new faculty additions to business schools during
the 1960s came from other disciplines. While this change in faculty
composition was welcomed by many critical of business schools (including the Foundation Reports), it brought with it yet a different set
of problems, still thought by some to be the final legacy of the
Foundation Reports. Since many of the newer faculty had received
no training at all in business (and some were unsympathetic to business problems in general), a growing gap began to develop between
business practitioners and business faculty. Indeed, by the end of
the decade the concerns regarding overemphasis on vocational concerns had been replaced by criticism that business programs were
becoming too esoteric and theoretical.

The 1960s also witnessed a definite shift in focus away from
undergraduate education toward graduate education. This shift to-

ward graduate work, accompanied by the addition of large numbers of faculty from the social sciences, mathematics, and engineering, elevated the status of the business school considerably within the university community.

The fact that business schools were largely unaffected by the cries for relevance on campus during the late 1960s can, in retrospect, be seen as evidence of their fortuitous positioning for the emergence of what has been labeled as the new vocationalism: the decade of the 1970s.

NEW VOCATIONALISM

It was during the late 1960s that enrollment in the newly arrived as well as the traditional professional school programs ex-

TABLE 4.1

Baccalaureate Degrees Awarded

Year	Graduates in All Disciplines	Business Graduates	Percentage of Business Graduates
1962	382,822	51,909	13.5
1965	492,984	62,999	12.7
1968	636,863	80,440	12.6
1971	846,110	116,709	13.7
1974	954,376	133,905	14.0
1977	928,228	153,762	16.5
1978	921,204	161,271	17.5
1979	931,340	175,420	18.8
1980	939,436	189,197	20.1

Source: Reprinted from National Center for Education Statistics, "Earned Degrees Conferred," AACSB Newsline 12, no. 1 (October 1981): 3, with permission of the American Assembly of Collegiate Schools of Business.

TABLE 4.2

Master's Degrees Awarded

Year	Graduates in All Disciplines	Business Graduates	Percentage of Business Graduates
1962	84,889	5,303	6.2
1965	112,195	6,585	7.0
1968	117,150	17,868	10.0
1971	321,486	26,654	11.6
1974	278,259	32,820	12.2
1977	318,241	46,650	14.4
1978	311,620	48,484	15.5
1979	302,075	50,646	16.6
1980	299,492	55,499	18.5

Source: Reprinted from National Center for Education Statistics, "Earned Degrees Conferred," AACSB Newsline 12, no. 1 (October 1981): 3, with permission of the American Assembly of Collegiate Schools of Business.

TABLE 4.3

Enrollment in Higher Education by Type of Institution

Institution	1974 (millions)	1979 (millions)	Percent Change
Universities	2,702	2,840	5.1
Other four-year	4,117	4,514	9.6
Two-year	3,404	4,217	23.9

Source: U.S., Department of Education, National Center for Education Statistics, Fall Enrollment in Higher Education (1979).

43

TABLE 4.4

Adult Education Enrollment, 1979/80 Noncredit Courses

	Universities	Other Four-Year	Two-Year	Public	Private	All Institutions
Business and management						
Accounting	25,161	15,927	32,032	59,154	13,966	73,120
Investments and securities	19,918	20,889	45,240	69,374	16,673	86,047
Marketing and purchasing	17,853	8,935	13,127	30,462	8,453	38,915
Real estate	55,668	36,148	102,951	165,081	29,686	194,767
Other	321,101	176,711	318,319	733,443	82,688	816,131
Occupational technologies						
Business and commerce	52,563	21,664	276,508	338,743	11,692	350,435
Data processing	5,317	3,319	32,101	34,508	6,229	40,737
Health and paramedical	38,618	28,846	355,429	385,882	37,011	422,893
Mechanical and engineering	20,386	36,521	421,036	466,842	11,101	477,943
Natural science	13,134	33,601	105,485	143,291	8,929	152,220
Public-service related	46,980	52,949	132,791	226,276	6,444	232,720
Other	337	325	6,926	7,588	0	7,588

Source: U.S., Department of Education, National Center for Education Statistics, Enrollment in Adult Education (1980).

TABLE 4.5

Enrollment in Institutions of Higher Education, 1963-80

Year	Enrollment (in millions)	Percentage of 18- to 24-Year-Olds Enrolled
1963	4,766	26.1
1965	5,921	29.2
1967	6,912	31.0
1969	8,005	33.7
1971	8,949	34.7
1973	9,602	36.4
1975	11,185	40.5
1977	11,286	39.5
1979	11,570	39.5
1980	11,940	40.5

Source: U.S., Department of Education, National Center for Education Statistics, Fall Enrollment in Higher Education (1980).

ploded. As noted by Cheit, the first indications of the new vocationalism were a doubling of law school enrollments from 1963 to 1973 and climbing rejection rates for applicants in medicine, dentistry, and architecture. The arrest of enrollment declines in engineering and pressures on business school enrollments signaled further proof of the appeal of job-related courses of study.[1]

The most notable shift toward business undergraduate enrollments lagged several years behind the expansion of M.B.A. enrollments. As shown in Tables 4.1 and 4.2 business degrees at both the undergraduate and graduate levels grew dramatically in both absolute and relative terms during the period between 1962 and 1980.

TABLE 4.6

AACSB Enrollment Trends
(in percent)

| | Enrollment | | Degrees Awarded, |
	1973	1980	1980
Undergraduate			
Men	70	49	56
Women	19	40	35
Minorities	11	11	9
M.B.A.			
Men	83	62	76
Women	11	31	25
Minorities	6	7	9

Source: Reprinted from National Center for Education Statistics, "Earned Degrees Conferred," AACSB Newsline 12, no. 1 (October 1981): 3, with permission of the American Assembly of Collegiate Schools of Business.

Two-year community colleges (heavily vocational) witnessed the greatest growth of all during this period, growing at a rate more than double that of four-year institutions (see Table 4.3). The growth of noncredit vocational courses was not restricted to community colleges, however; significant growth occurred at universities as well (see Table 4.4).

Undoubtedly, much of the explanation for this increased emphasis on vocationalism can be found in the fact that increasing numbers of individuals from the baby-boom generation were being graduated, saturating many job markets and leading to competition for "marketable skills" as well as a college degree. From 1963 to 1980 the percentage of 18- to 24-year-olds enrolled in colleges increased dramatically. This—coupled with the increased number of persons in the 18- to 24-year-old age group—created a double effect on enrollments, leading to 1980 enrollments that were 250 percent larger than in 1963 (see Table 4.5).

The value shifts reflective of the "me" generation were like-wise conducive to the development of career-oriented business school programs. Students increasingly began to see practical and salable business skills as the short-run means to achieve their life-style goals. Women students, especially, began to switch their career plans (and therefore majors) into business. By 1980 women represented 40 percent of all undergraduate business students and 31 percent of all M.B.A. students at AACSB accredited schools (see Tables 4.6 and 4.7). During this same period part-time enrollment in business programs began to increase, reaching 18 percent of all

TABLE 4.7

Business Degrees Awarded in 1980

Degree	Institution		
	Public	Private	Total
Bachelor's			
Men	79,091	46,331	125,422
Women	42,033	21,742	63,775
Total	121,124	68,073	189,197
Master's			
Men	18,430	24,687	43,117
Women	5,461	6,921	12,382
Total	23,891	31,608	55,499
Doctor's			
Men	482	199	681
Women	85	34	119
Total	567	233	800

Source: U.S., Department of Education, National Center for Education Statistics (1980).

TABLE 4.8

Marketing Major Career Paths

Advertising Management Emphasis	Marketing Management Emphasis	Marketing Research Emphasis	Physical Distribution Emphasis
Principles of Marketing	Principles of Marketing	Principles of Marketing	Principles of Marketing
Principles of Advertising	Marketing Research or Quantita-	Marketing Research Methods	Physical Distribution
Marketing Research Methods	tive Marketing Analysis	Consumer Behavior	Principles of Advertising,
Consumer Behavior	Principles of Advertising,	Research Problems in Marketing	Creative Motivation in Market-
Advertising Management	Creative Motivation in Market-	Marketing Problems	ing, or Consumer Behavior
Marketing Problems	ing, or Consumer Behavior	Marketing Electives (2)	Quantitative Marketing Analysis
Marketing Elective (1)	Industrial Marketing		Management of Physical Dis-
	Marketing Problems		tribution Operations
	Marketing Electives (2)		Marketing Problems
			Marketing Elective (1)

Sales Management Emphasis	International Marketing Emphasis	Retailing Emphasis
Principles of Marketing	Principles of Marketing	Principles of Marketing
Creative Motivation in Marketing	Principles of Advertising,	Principles of Advertising
Marketing Research Methods	Creative Motivation in Market-	Principles of Retailing
Consumer Behavior	ing, or Consumer Behavior	Marketing Research Methods
Management of the Sale Force	Marketing Research Methods	Consumer Behavior
Marketing Problems	International Marketing	Marketing Problems in
Marketing Elective (1)	Marketing Problems	Retail Sector
	Marketing Electives (2)	Marketing Problems

Source: Taken from California State University-Fullerton, Department of Marketing, Marketing, Marketing and U (Fullerton: California State University, 1975), pp. 9-10.

undergraduate students and 55 percent of all graduate students in AACSB schools.

During the early 1970s a number of business schools (primarily larger state universities) began developing highly specialized "career tract" programs <u>within</u> each functional discipline. An example of the extent of such specialization is shown in Table 4. 8. This program was developed in 1974 by the Marketing Department at California State University, Fullerton.

Such specialized curricula were generally popularly received both by students seeking an advantage in the job market and by faculty feeling increased professional pressure to further specialize their teaching and research activities within rapidly expanding functional areas. Indeed, the technologically inspired trend toward functional specialization became one of the major legacies of the business schools of the 1970s.

RANKING THE TOP BUSINESS SCHOOLS

The growing popularity of the business school on campus also led to another popular exercise, namely, a lively debate over which business schools were the "best." Strong interest in this question began to range beyond the confines of faculty discussion in the late 1960s and especially the 1970s as a result of growth in student enrollments, proliferation of M. B. A. programs nationally, and the accompanying marketplace competition for jobs.

While the task of accurately ranking business schools remains fraught with methodological problems, this did not deter a number of studies from attempting to sort out the business school "pecking order." During the 1970s M. B. A. magazines conducted several surveys of both their readers (M. B. A. graduates) and business school deans in order to investigate the relative quality and employment value of leading graduate business schools.[2] Likewise studies of graduate education (including business) were undertaken by Cartter[3] and reported in the <u>Chronicle of Higher Education</u>,[4] and by Gourman.[5] The results of these studies are summarized in Table 4. 9. Note that the rankings of the various universities are roughly comparable across all four studies. While there is no general agreement concerning the appropriate method of rating business schools, there is general agreement as to which are the best. As pointed out by Hunger and Wheelen in a yet-to-be-discussed study, seven of the twelve schools listed (and all three top-rated schools) were exclusively graduate business schools.[6]

TABLE 4.9

Comparative Rankings of Graduate Business Schools

Institution	M. B. A. Magazine	Chronicle	"Cartter"	Gourman
Stanford University	1	1	1	4
Harvard University	2	2	2	1
University of Chicago	3	3	4	3
MIT (Sloan)	4	8	3	5
University of Pennsylvania (Wharton)	5	4	7	2
Carnegie-Mellon University	6	—	5	7
Northwestern University	7	5	9	—
UCLA	8	11	8	8
Dartmouth University (Tuck)	9	—	—	—
University of Michigan	10	10	—	10
Columbia University	11	12	11	6
University of California (Berkeley)	12	9	6	—

Note: Missing figures indicate that the institution was not ranked among the top 12 in that particular survey.

Sources: Steven Ross, "Ranking the Business Schools," M. B. A. Magazine, December 1977, pp. 19-24; Malcolm Scully, "The Well-known Universities Lead in the Rating of Faculty Reputations," Chronicle of Higher Education, January 15, 1979; "The Cartter Report on the Leading Schools of Education, Law and Business," Change, February 1977, pp. 44-48; Jack Gourman, The Gourman Report—A Ranking of American and International Universities (Los Angeles: National Education Standards, 1980), p. 16.

Ratings of undergraduate business programs have been much less common. The findings of two of the latest studies are shown in Table 4. 10. Hunger and Wheelen surveyed deans among AACSB schools with accredited undergraduate programs, senior personnel executives among key industrial firm groupings, and directors of AACSB accredited M. B. A. programs. [7] In the second study, Gourman made use of questionnaires sent to university administrators, along with various other secondary data evaluations of institutional quality. [8] The rankings of top undergraduate business programs were quite similar among deans, personnel executives, and M. B. A. directors within the Hunger-Wheelen study, and between respondents in their study and those in the Gourman study.

Hunger and Wheelen also investigated the criteria used by the respondents to evaluate the schools listed. As shown in Table 4. 11, the reputation of the faculty was the overwhelming factor in explaining the ratings of all three respondent groups. Further, when asked whether these criteria would be the same when rating graduate business schools, 61 percent of the deans and 78 percent of the personnel executives said yes. [9] As concluded by Hunger and Wheelen, "There appears to be little or no differentiation in people's minds between undergraduate and graduate programs."[10] Further evidence for this conclusion is found in the fact that five exclusively graduate business schools (Harvard, Stanford, Columbia, Chicago, and Northwestern) received enough response to be ranked among the top ten undergraduate schools as well. [11]

The Hunger-Wheelen study also sought to determine how the survey respondents perceived the relative importance of different undergraduate business education objectives. As shown in Table 4. 12, the importance rankings for all three groups are reasonably similar. Regarding the focus of undergraduate programs, Hunger and Wheelen concluded that

the basic points of agreement on most important and least important objectives suggest that all respondents felt that undergraduate business education needed to focus primarily on the "basics," e. g. developing logical thinking and an understanding of foundation subject areas. Knowledge acquisition of business principles and especially of current business practices were not viewed as critical as learning the skills necessary to approach and deal with problems. Since the respondents tended not to view training for specific positions or in specific functional areas to be of great importance, one might assume that

TABLE 4.10

Comparative Rankings of Undergraduate Business Schools

Institution	Dean	Personnel Executive	M. B. A. Director	Gourman
University of Pennsylvania (Wharton)	1	1	1	1
University of Michigan	2	2	3	4
University of California (Berkeley)	3	5–8	5	5
Indiana University	4	4	2	3
University of Texas (Austin)	5–6	9	6–7	9
University of Illinois (Urbana)	5–6	5–8	4	6
Ohio State University	7	10–11	6–7	8
University of Virginia (McIntire)	8	3	8	10
New York University	9	5–8	—	7
MIT	10–12	5–8	—	2
University of Notre Dame	10–12	—	—	—
University of Washington (Seattle)	10–12	—	—	—
University of Southern California	—	10–11	9–10	—
Michigan State University	—	—	9–10	—
Purdue University	—	—	—	8

Note: Missing figures indicate that the institution was not ranked among the top 12 in that particular survey. Double numbers indicate ties for those positions.

Sources: For data in columns headed "Dean," "Personnel Executive," and "M. B. A. Director," source is J. David Hunger and Thomas L. Wheelen, An Assessment of Undergraduate Business Education in the United States (Charlottesville, Va.: McIntire School of Commerce Foundation), p. 7. For data in last column, source is Jack Gourman, The Gourman Report—A Ranking of American and International Universities (Los Angeles: National Education Standards, 1980), p. 14.

TABLE 4.11

Criteria Used to Select Best Schools

Criteria	Dean		Executive		Director	
	Percent Mentioned	Rank	Percent Mentioned	Rank	Percent Mentioned	Rank
Faculty reputation	61	1	57	1	59	1
Academic reputation	33	2-4	33	4	28	5
Quality of students	33	2-4	15	5	30	4
Curriculum	33	2-4	38	3	35	2
Financial resources	31	5	—	—	—	—
Performance of graduates	—	—	43	2	33	3

Note: Double numbers indicate ties for those positions.

Source: Reprinted with permission from J. David Hunger and Thomas L. Wheelen, An Assessment of Undergraduate Business Education in the United States (Charlottesville, Va.: McIntire School of Commerce Foundation, 1980), p. 8. Copyright © 1980 by McIntire School of Commerce Foundation.

TABLE 4.12

Ranking of Objectives of Undergraduate Business Education

Objective	Dean	Personnel Executive	M. B. A. Director
Training to develop understanding of political, social, and economic environment of business	1	6-7	6
Training in basic subjects applicable to business, for example, economics, psychology, English, mathematics	2-5	4	3-5
Training to develop problem-solving abilities	2-5	2-3	1-2
Training in techniques of application of basic subjects of business, for example, forecasting, personnel, report writing, statistics	2-5	1	3-5
Training in business principles, for example, managerial economics	6	5	3-5
Training for responsible general management positions, for example, vice-president, production division	7	10	10
Training for general work in specific functional areas of business, for example, sales, sales management	8	8	7
Training in current business practices, for example, salary administration procedures	9	9	9
Training for specific positions common to several businesses, for example, cost accountant	10	6-7	8
Training for specific positions in given industries, for example, store manager for supermarket	11	11	11

Note: Double numbers indicate ties for those positions.

Source: J. David Hunger and Thomas L. Wheelen, An Assessment of Undergraduate Business Education in the United States (Charlottesville, Va.: McIntire School of Commerce Foundation, 1980), p. 11.

this type of education was thought of as more appropriate for in-house or on-the-job training than for business schools. [12]

In commenting on the differences in educational objectives for graduate versus undergraduate business programs perceived by study respondents, Hunger and Wheelen further commented that

it appears, in conclusion, that undergraduate business education is expected to do many different kinds of things for many different kinds of people. Students want the program to educate them, but especially to provide them with the skills necessary to obtain an entry level job so they can eventually move into general management. Faculty want the same things, but also feel a need to emphasize basic subjects as well. Deans are most concerned with general education; whereas, personnel executives and MBA directors are also concerned with basic skills and training for specific positions. Graduate business programs do not appear to have this problem. The emphasis is upon those processing skills necessary for successful general management. Undergraduate programs, however, must attempt as best they can to emphasize the general education basics and teach the skills necessary for entry level as well as upper level management positions. [13]

Yet another measure of difference between undergraduate business education and graduate education can be found in the marketplace values placed on degrees granted from different institutions and on a B.A. versus an M.B.A. degree. The rising value of the M.B.A. during the 1960s and 1970s can be seen in its relative increase in value over the B.A. degree during the same period. In 1965 the average M.B.A. salary was 27 percent greater than that for a B.A.; by 1977 this difference had increased to 47 percent. [14]

By 1979 this discrepancy was reportedly 61 percent. However, it was pointed out that large differences between top-rated and second-tier M.B.A. schools existed. In 1970 nearly 50 percent of all M.B.A.'s were produced by the top 20 schools; by 1979 this figure had dropped to 15 percent. [15]

Salary gaps between graduates of various M.B.A. programs were also noticeable. Harvard M.B.A. graduates continued to outpace all others in starting salaries, surpassing even other top-rated schools by as much as 25 percent up until the mid-1970s. By 1977 several other top business schools began to close this gap, with Stanford's M.B.A.'s reporting starting salaries essentially equal to those of Harvard. [16]

AN UNEASY PEACE

The ever-growing popularity of the business school among students, coupled with its increasing specialization, made for an uneasy relationship between the business school and the liberal arts college. Business schools have seldom enjoyed full privileges and status within the university community. (It has often been pointed out that even at Harvard the business school had been strategically positioned across the Charles River from the main campus.) However, the obvious market popularity of business schools, the increasingly competitive entry-level job market, and students' preoccupations with getting good jobs have created an interesting marriage between the liberal and the useful on campus.

While recognizing (albeit begrudgingly) the value of the business school as a way to legitimize college education to a generation of pragmatists, most campus administrators were notably uneasy with the idea of allowing business schools further access to the seats of power. Indeed, many senior administrators saw swelling business school enrollments as an easy way to subsidize more costly university programs by adjusting full-time equivalent student (FTES) ratios to increase business school classes in order to compensate for declining enrollments elsewhere on campus.

The mid-1970s also witnessed a concerted effort by those in the liberal arts to challenge the conventional wisdom that those with liberal arts backgrounds were at a disadvantage in the job market. Several studies tracking the career success of university liberal arts graduates were undertaken and used to demonstrate the usefulness of liberal education (especially in obtaining long-run career goals). [17] This debate over the relative merits of various educational backgrounds as preparation for business has continued uninterrupted to this day.

INTERNAL CHANGES IN THE BUSINESS SCHOOL

Along with the phenomenal growth of business schools during the last decade came a number of internal problems. Growth brought a change in the composition as well as the size of business school student populations. Business schools began attracting increasing numbers of quality students from across campus (both male and female).

This reversal of the long-standing tendency of business schools to attract students of lesser ability (cited by the Foundation Reports) was noticeable at both the undergraduate and graduate levels. To wit, business professors teaching graduate courses began to commonly encounter students in their classes already possessing advanced degrees in science and engineering and, to a lesser degree, the liberal arts. These changes in the student body necessitated a continual upgrading of the business curriculum.

Such changes were not felt equally by all business schools, however, and while the better schools prospered from such changes, other less attractive business schools were left to deal not primarily with quality issues but, rather, with problems of processing larger and larger numbers of students of mediocre abilities. The growth of the 1970s also strained faculty resources to the limit. As student enrollments grew dramatically, the supply of business professors (especially new doctorates) fell off substantially. This mismatch of supply and demand (which has become even more acute in the 1980s) in turn led to an overreliance at many business schools on part-time lecturers, increased class sizes, and concern over controlling the quality of program output.

The concern over program quality was expressed by business executives as well as academic administrators, as evidenced by the involvement of the AACSB over the last few years in attempting to define, measure, and control the output of business school programs.[18] Standardized testing of M.B.A. student skills was one proposed way to control program output. Such tests were to measure not only cognitive skills in areas such as accounting, finance, quantitative methods, and so forth, but also noncognitive skills such as leadership and ability to deal with job risk and stress. The American Assembly of Collegiate Schools of Business panels comprised of deans and businessmen developed a list of 19 attributes, which were reduced to the following six categories:

1. Administrative skills (including decision-making ability)
2. Performance stability (including tolerance of uncertainty)
3. Work motivation (including energy level)
4. Interpersonal skills (including leadership)
5. Values of business (primarily ethics)
6. General mental ability[19]

Currently, the AACSB is wrestling with developing measures of these attributes that are amenable to the testing of M.B.A. students. Arguments continue not only over measurement issues but also over whether some of these qualities can be taught in business schools at all.

Given the present-day popularity of business schools on campus and the growing concerns among business communities concerning the output of such programs, a study was undertaken to better understand the extent of differences in the perceptions of academic and business administrators regarding the appropriate university training for careers in business. The following chapter details the specific objectives, methodology, and findings of this study, which was funded in large part by a grant from the Shelby Cullom Davis Educational Foundation.

NOTES

1. Earl Cheit, The Useful Arts and the Liberal Tradition (New York: McGraw-Hill), pp. 4-5.

2. Steven Ross, "Ranking the Business Schools," M.B.A. Magazine, December 1977, pp. 19-24.

3. "The Cartter Report on the Leading Schools of Education, Law and Business," Change, February 1977, pp. 44-48.

4. Malcolm Scully, "The Well-known Universities Lead in the Rating of Faculty Reputations," Chronicle of Higher Education, January 15, 1979, p. 7.

5. Jack Gourman, The Gourman Report—A Rating of American and International Universities (Los Angeles: National Education Standards, 1980).

6. J. David Hunger and Thomas L. Wheelen, An Assessment of Undergraduate Business Education in the United States (Charlottesville, Va.: McIntire School of Commerce Foundation, 1980), p. 2.

7. Ibid., p. 4.

8. Gourman, Gourman Report.

9. Hunger and Wheelen, Assessment, p. 8.

10. Ibid.

11. Ibid., p. 5.

12. Ibid., p. 12.

13. Ibid., p. 19.

14. "School, Geography Effect on M.B.A.'s Level of Income," Washington Post, January 8, 1978.

15. "MBA Recipients, Once Eagerly Sought, Now Eagerly Seek Jobs in Tight Market," Wall Street Journal, November 2, 1979.

16. Ibid.

17. P. Abrego, "From Liberal Arts to a Career," Journal of College Placement 38 (Winter 1978): 60-74; J. Chasin and G. Benson, "Entry-Level Positions: Do Business Schools Really Give an Advantage?" Journal of College Placement 37 (Fall 1976): 73-77; and H. B. Sagen, "Careers, Competencies and Liberal Education," Liberal Education 65 (1979): 150-66.

18. "A Plan to Rate Business Schools by Testing Students," Business Week, November 19, 1979, pp. 171, 174.

19. Business Week, November 19, 1979, p. 174.

5

PERCEPTIONS OF THE BUSINESS SCHOOL AMONG ACADEMIC AND BUSINESS ADMINISTRATORS

Recent years have witnessed a number of potentially conflicting trends in the education of students for careers in business. First is the aforementioned increase in the enrollments in business school programs (with an accompanying decrease in liberal arts enrollments).[1] A second trend has been a greater orientation within business school curricula toward entry-level career training—evidenced by the development of career-path curriculum programs, increased specialization in department offerings by most business schools, and the trend toward offering a Master of Science in Business degree as an alternative to the traditional M.B.A.[2]

Accompanying the above developments, however, have been additional trends that may foretell trouble for business schools. One of these trends is the increasing dissatisfaction of many business leaders with the product of many business school programs—and a concurrent call for broader perspectives in training young people for their future roles in the business world.[3] This concern is especially acute given yet a fourth trend, the saturation of the market with M.B.A.'s; M.B.A. program output has more than doubled in less than a decade.[4]

A final trend, which is especially curious to business school department administrators, is a 35 percent relative decline in market share for marketing majors (expressed as a percentage of total business school degrees granted since 1973).[5] This trend, despite the clamor for training with more "real-world relevance" from many employees, leaves many in marketing departments (reputed to be among the most applied and practical of business disciplines) somewhat confused and bewildered.

While business school enrollments continue to swell, changes in the demographics of the educational market, signs of nearing market saturation levels, and changes in the challenges facing business—which call for greater social awareness and sensitivity to a broader range of decision criteria—all signal the need to resist complacency and continue to develop programs that better match the evolving needs of the business community. Nowhere is such a posture more appropriate than within the discipline of marketing, where the above-mentioned loss of market share has been paralleled by a rather dismal importance rating (relative to other business disciplines, namely, accounting and finance) by both students and businessmen.[6]

How can the above-mentioned trends be rationalized? Are they necessarily inconsistent? Where is the focus on careerism headed? Does business really prefer functional specialization over a liberal arts background in hiring employees? Just how discrepant are the attitudes of various administrators concerning the proper balance of career training versus liberal education? What educational backgrounds or combination of backgrounds are preferred by business?

In an attempt to provide answers to these and other important questions, a study was undertaken to compare the attitudes of deans of schools of liberal arts with those of business school deans, university placement directors, and corporate personnel directors to determine the extent to which these attitudes diverge and lead to different levels of involvement with various types of joint programs (internships, faculty exchange programs, joint majors, and the like), all of which attempt to bridge the gap between the traditional role of university education and today's demands for "marketplace relevance."

METHODOLOGY

This study proposed to identify and measure the magnitude of perceptual differences separating academia and the business world. The research design was partly exploratory and partly statistical.

Primary data were gathered through a questionnaire mailed to a stratified national sample of deans (liberal arts and business), university placement directors, and corporate executives. The questionnaire employed a forced-choice format utilizing a seven-point scale to measure perceptions and attitudes and a compact three-point scale to elicit degree of involvement in various activities. Open-

TABLE 5.1

Distribution of Respondents

Position	Number of Respondents	Percentage of Total
Liberal arts dean	87	26
Business school dean	76	23
University placement director	50	15
Corporate personnel director	120	36

TABLE 5.2

Years Experience in Present Position
(percent of total within each position)

Position	Less than 1 Year	1 Year	2-5 Years	5-10 Years	Greater than 10 Years
Liberal arts dean	5	17	37	30	12
Business school dean	8	22	38	20	12
University placement director	4	12	36	26	22
Business personnel director	4	23	46	12	15

Chi square value = 17.8
Degrees of freedom = 12
Significance level = not significant

Note: Because of rounding, percentages may not total 100.

ended questions were included to solicit suggestions from deans for bridging the gap between the needs of students and those of their eventual employers. An overall response rate of slightly over 41 percent of mailed questionnaires was attained.

The sampling universe for the academic subjects consisted of all those institutions listed in the 1977/78 edition of Accredited Institutions of Postsecondary Education and the Fifteenth Edition of the College Bluebook. A sample of 250 deans in liberal arts schools, 125 deans of business schools, and 125 placement directors was chosen. These three academic roles were sampled in the same institution where possible, in an attempt to hold environmental effects constant and uncover actual differences, if any, in perceptual focus among the three educator groups. One-half of the institutions sampled had a business program; the remainder did not. The sampling universe was stratified by size of university (and school), geographic location, type of control (public or private), religious relationship (where appropriate), and level of degree offered. A 42 percent response rate (210 returns) was secured from the academic units after two mailings.

The sample frame for the business firms consisted of all those firms listed in the 1979 College Placement Annual and the Professional Edition of the Career Opportunity Index. In addition, a group of California-based firms, which were listed in business directories for that state and which would be available for personal interviews if necessary, was included. This universe was stratified on the basis of company size, industry (or product group), and geographic location in order to investigate differential perceptions along these dimensions. Corporate personnel officers returned 120 usable questionnaires (after a follow-up mailing) from an initial mailing of 300, for a response rate of 40 percent.

A distribution of respondents among the four groups is presented in Table 5.1. Profiles of respondents are provided in Tables 5.2 through 5.16. Table 5.2 shows that there were no significant differences in times spent in their present positions among the four groups of respondents. In each case over two-thirds of the respondents had been in their present positions two years or more and, therefore, hopefully represented a knowledgeable group from which to elicit opinions concerning careers and education.

As expected, Tables 5.3 and 5.4 show significantly different background experiences in business and education among respondent groups. Business personnel directors and liberal arts deans possessed nearly opposite backgrounds, with business school deans and university placement directors representing a mixture of business and educational experiences.

TABLE 5.3

Years of Business Experience
(percent of total respondents within each position)

Position	Less than 1 Year	1 Year	2-5 Years	5-10 Years	Greater than 10 Years
Liberal arts dean	74	3	12	7	5
Business school dean	25	8	38	16	13
University placement director	48	2	22	14	14
Business personnel director	2	0	13	24	61

Chi square value = 194.7
Degrees of freedom = 12
Significance level = .01

Note: Because of rounding, percentages may not total 100.

TABLE 5.4

Experience in Education
(percent of total respondents within each position)

Position	Less than 1 Year	1 Year	2-5 Years	5-10 Years	Greater than 10 Years
Liberal arts dean	5	0	2	1	92
Business school dean	5	0	5	20	70
University placement director	6	2	4	22	66
Business personnel director	63	5	20	4	8

Chi square value = 223.4
Degrees of freedom = 12
Significance level = .01

Table 5.5 shows significant educational differences, with the vast majority of deans being terminally qualified, most university placement directors possessing master's degrees, and most business personnel directors possessing bachelor's or master's degrees.

Table 5.6 shows that two-thirds of all liberal arts deans responding were trained in the liberal arts, with most of the remainder having science or education degrees. While nearly two-thirds of business deans were trained in business disciplines, a significant number (22 percent) had come through liberal arts (economics was included in liberal arts for purposes of classification). University placement directors had predominantly education degrees. Interestingly, business personnel directors were as likely to have liberal arts degrees as business degrees. The educational backgrounds of the respondents are not only interesting in terms of illustrating various career paths but also must be kept in mind for their moderating influences on the respondents' perceptions of the "appropriate" educational preparation for a business career, as investigated in this study.

Using the year in which the respondents' final degrees were obtained (Table 5.7) as a surrogate for age and experience, university placement directors and business personnel directors were shown to be the youngest and oldest, respectively. Liberal arts and business school deans were very similar in this regard.

No significant differences in the geographic locations of university respondents were found (see Table 5.8).

Table 5.9 shows that liberal arts deans are drawn broadly from public, private, and religiously affiliated institutions, while the business school deans and university placement directors who responded were primarily from public institutions.

Significant differences were also found in the sizes of the respondents' employing institutions (see Table 5.10). While business school deans and university placement directors were primarily from medium-sized to large institutions, liberal arts deans were divided equally among institutions of all sizes.

Related to the above, approximately one-third of the liberal arts colleges and universities in the sample offered only bachelor's degrees, while most business school deans and placement directors represented colleges and universities offering primarily master's and doctoral degrees (see Table 5.11).

Table 5.12 shows that no business degrees were offered at the colleges or universities of over 40 percent of the liberal arts deans in the sample. This must be kept in mind later when examining the involvement levels of respondents in joint-type programs.

TABLE 5.5

Educational Background
(percent of total respondents within each position)

Position	None	High School	2 Years of College	Degrees Earned		
				Bachelor's	Master's	Ph. D.
Liberal arts dean	0	0	0	0	8	92
Business school dean	4	0	0	1	12	83
University placement director	2	0	0	2	72	24
Business personnel director	4	1	1	54	40	0

Chi square value = 233.4
Degrees of freedom = 12
Significance level = .01

TABLE 5.6

College Major
(percent of total respondents within each position)

Position	No Response	Liberal Arts	Business	Science	Technology	Other Professional	Education	Other
Liberal arts dean	0	66	2	17	0	1	10	3
Business school dean	5	22	63	0	3	4	3	0
University placement director	2	8	18	0	2	2	68	0
Business personnel director	6	42	41	2	3	3	4	2

Chi square value = 246.4
Degree of freedom = 21
Significance level = .01

Note: Because of rounding, percentages may not total 100.

TABLE 5.7

Year Degree Obtained
(percent of total respondents within each position)

Position	Before 1950	1950–59	1960–69	1970–75	1976–79
Liberal arts dean	8	26	38	22	4
Business school dean	7	17	49	24	4
University placement director	6	12	34	28	20
Business personnel director	16	10	29	25	19

Chi square value = 147.4
Degrees of freedom = 12
Significance level = .01

Note: Because of rounding, percentages may not total 100.

TABLE 5.8

Geographic Distribution of University Respondents
(percent of total respondents within each position)

Position	East	South	Midwest	West	California
Liberal arts dean	23	17	36	13	12
Business school dean	19	20	33	19	9
University placement director	16	22	34	18	10

Chi square value = 2. 6
Degrees of freedom = 8
Significance level = not significant

Note: Because of rounding, percentages may not total 100.

TABLE 5.9

Types of Institutions of Academic Respondents
(percent of total respondents within each position)

Position	No Response	Public	Private	Religious Affiliation
Liberal arts dean	4	42	23	31
Business school dean	0	64	18	19
University placement director	0	76	14	10

Chi square value = 19. 4
Degrees of freedom = 6
Significance level = . 01

TABLE 5.10

Enrollments of Institutions of Academic Respondents
(percent of total respondents within each position)

Position	0–1,000	1,000–2,500	2,500–5,000	5,000–15,000	15,000–50,000
Liberal arts dean	17	20	17	30	16
Business school dean	1	5	13	43	37
University placement director	0	0	0	40	60

Note: Because of rounding, percentages may not total 100.

TABLE 5.11

Highest Degrees Granted by Academic Respondents' Institutions
(percent of total respondents within each position)

Position	Bachelor's	Master's	Ph.D.
Liberal arts dean	32	33	35
Business school dean	8	33	59
University placement director	10	22	68

Chi square value = 25.3
Degrees of freedom = 4
Significance level = .01

TABLE 5.12

Highest Business Degree Offered by Respondents' Institutions
(percent of total respondents within each position)

Position	None	Bachelor's	Master's	Ph. D.
Liberal arts dean	41	14	38	7
Business school dean	3	16	67	15
University placement director	4	32	48	16

Chi square value = 55.4
Degrees of freedom = 6
Significance level = .01

Note: Because of rounding, percentages may not total 100.

TABLE 5.13

Highest Level of Business Accreditation
at Respondents' Institutions
(percent of total respondents within each position)

Position	None	Bachelor's	Master's
Liberal arts dean	73	6	21
Business school dean	39	20	41
University placement director	28	21	51

Chi square value = 30.4
Degrees of freedom = 4
Significance level = .01

TABLE 5.14

Geographic Distribution of Corporate Personnel Directors

Region	Percentage of Total
East	12
South	4
Midwest	14
West	18
California	52

TABLE 5.15

Industry Background of Corporate Personnel Directors

Background	Percentage of Total
Agriculture	8
Mining	3
Manufacturing	48
Transportation/Utilities	9
Retailing	8
Finance/Real estate	11
Services	10
Construction	3

TABLE 5.16

Corporate Structure of Corporate Personnel Directors

	Percentage of Total
Size of firm (number of employees)	
Under 100	4
100–500	17
500–2,500	34
2,500–10,000	22
Over 10,000	24
Organizational unit	
Headquarters	47
Subsidiary	53

Table 5.13 presents information on the accreditation of business programs among responding institutions. It appears that among liberal arts schools, few undergraduate programs in business exist, and undergraduate business accreditation nearly always accompanies or precedes graduate business accreditation. Undergraduate business programs (both accredited and nonaccredited) were much more common among business school and university placement respondents.

Tables 5.14 through 5.16 summarize background data on corporate personnel directors included in the study. Among personnel directors, the majority were purposively drawn from California in order that personal interviews could be obtained for a follow-up study. Nearly one-half of the respondents were from the manufacturing sector and were distributed rather evenly by size of firm. Approximately one-half of the personnel directors responding were from corporate headquarters and the other one-half from subsidiary operating companies.

In general, the final stratified sample of 333 respondents represented a good cross section of administrators who dealt with questions both of academic program content and of marketplace relevance.

The following section details the findings of the survey regarding respondents' views on the appropriate present and future roles of business education.

VIEWS ON CAREER TRAINING

The profiles presented in Figure 5.1 compare the perceptions of the four groups surveyed (liberal arts deans, business school deans, university placement directors, and corporate personnel directors) regarding the relative emphasis that universities and colleges should place on career training versus liberal arts. Statistically significant differences in the views of the four groups were uncovered for each of the seven measures of liberalism versus vocationalism investigated.

Responses to statement 1 showed (as might be expected) that liberal arts deans continue to value the perspective of a broad educational program; an increasing degree of indifference toward the liberal arts was exhibited by business deans, university placement directors, and business personnel directors, respectively. Responses to statement 2 evidenced a common concern across all four groups that basic and interpersonal skills are not addressed to a sufficient degree in any collegiate programs.

Part of the underlying reason for this dissatisfaction could be found in the responses to the third statement, which show a clear disagreement between academic deans and both business personnel and university placement directors concerning the role of education in career preparation and training. It appears that academic deans (business as well as liberal arts) do not see career preparation as a major part of their role as educators, while corporate personnel and university placement directors do see career preparation as central.

Reactions to statement 4, likewise, indicated that a substantial perceptual discrepancy existed between deans and corporate personnel and university placement directors concerning the present adequacy of educational programs in preparing students for the job market.

Statement 5 showed concern with potential overemphasis on specialization or career training to be especially acute among liberal arts deans. Statements 6 and 7 evidenced a significantly greater interest in career training among business personnel and university placement directors.

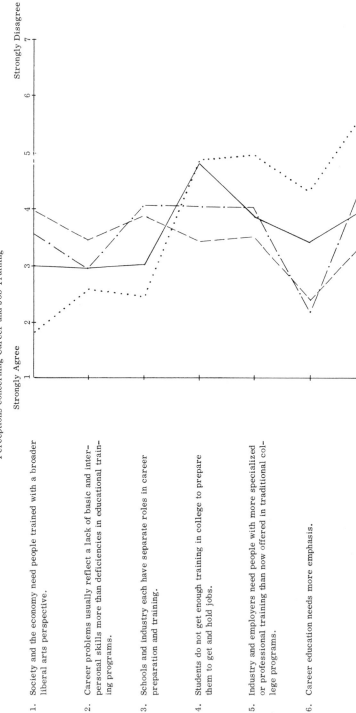

FIGURE 5.1

Perceptions concerning Career and Job Training

Strongly Agree   Strongly Disagree

1. Society and the economy need people trained with a broader
    liberal arts perspective.

2. Career problems usually reflect a lack of basic and inter-
    personal skills more than deficiencies in educational train-
    ing programs.

3. Schools and industry each have separate roles in career
    preparation and training.

4. Students do not get enough training in college to prepare
    them to get and hold jobs.

5. Industry and employers need people with more specialized
    or professional training than now offered in traditional col-
    lege programs.

6. Career education needs more emphasis.

7. College degrees (especially in liberal arts) are overvalued.

Code: ••••• = liberal arts deans, ———— = business school deans, — • — = university placement directors, — — — = corporate personnel directors.

It appears that much of the dissatisfaction on the part of students and employers, referenced earlier, can be explained by the significant discrepancies shown in Figure 5.1. Not only was there disagreement regarding the necessary preparation for business careers but also concerning the degree to which universities should be involved in this process at all.

Career Program Involvement

A closer examination of joint business–university involvement in career programs (including cooperative education, university and/or company-sponsored seminars and workshops, and continuing-education programs focusing on business) uncovered generally limited participation among those surveyed.

TABLE 5.17

Involvement in Cooperative Programs: Work/Study
Alternating Semesters
(in percent)

	Involvement		
Position	None	Limited	Major
Liberal arts dean	39	51	10
Business school dean	38	45	16
University placement director	20	46	34
Business personnel director	36	51	13

Chi square value = 16.8
Degrees of freedom = 6
Significance level = .01

Note: Because of rounding, percentages may not total 100.

TABLE 5.18

Involvement in Cooperative Programs: Work/Study Concurrently
(in percent)

Position	Involvement		
	None	Limited	Major
Liberal arts dean	11	72	18
Business school dean	16	57	27
University placement director	8	58	33
Business personnel director	22	60	18

Chi square value = 13.0
Degrees of freedom = 6
Significance level = .05

Note: Because of rounding, percentages may not total 100.

Significant differences in respondent involvement in cooperative education programs were found for both work/study programs, which alternated semesters, and for those programs in which students worked in a cooperative program concurrent with taking other university courses (see Tables 5.17 and 5.18). Cooperative programs that ran concurrent with classes were clearly more popular. Significant differences in involvement were also found to be a function of the size of the university and the level of degree offered. Larger universities and those offering Ph.D. and masters' degrees were more active in management development and joint company-university seminars and workshops. In contrast, involvement with cooperative education programs was greater among small (under 25,000 eenrollment) liberal arts schools than among larger schools.

Significant differences in respondent participation in joint university-business seminars were also uncovered (see Tables 5.19 through 5.21). As was expected, involvement levels were highest

TABLE 5.19

Participation in School-Sponsored Seminars and Workshops
(in percent)

Position	Involvement		
	None	Limited	Major
Liberal arts dean	8	66	26
Business school dean	4	54	42
University placement director	2	60	38
Business personnel director	18	68	14

Chi square value = 33.2
Degrees of freedom = 6
Significance level = .01

TABLE 5.20

Participation in Company-Sponsored Seminars
(in percent)

Position	Involvement		
	None	Limited	Major
Liberal arts dean	24	71	5
Business school dean	21	63	16
University placement director	15	67	19
Business personnel director	20	50	29

Chi square value = 21.9
Degrees of freedom = 6
Significance level = .01

Note: Because of rounding, percentages may not total 100.

TABLE 5.21

Participation in Government-Sponsored Seminars
(in percent)

Position	Involvement		
	None	Limited	Major
Liberal arts dean	40	57	4
Business school dean	38	58	4
University placement director	29	65	6
Business personnel director	41	53	6

Chi square value = 2.9
Degrees of freedom = 6
Significance level = not significant

Note: Because of rounding, percentages may not total 100.

TABLE 5.22

Participation in Management Development through Continuing Education
(in percent)

Position	Involvement		
	None	Limited	Major
Liberal arts dean	27	47	26
Business school dean	3	51	46
University placement director	12	62	26
Business personnel director	6	36	58

Chi square value = 48.5
Degrees of freedom = 6
Significance level = .01

TABLE 5.23

Participation in Career Education through Continuing Education
(in percent)

Position	Involvement		
	None	Limited	Major
Liberal arts dean	21	54	25
Business school dean	22	63	15
University placement director	22	58	20
Business personnel director	8	67	24

Chi square value = 12.5
Degrees of freedom = 6
Significance level = .05

Note: Because of rounding, percentages may not total 100.

TABLE 5.24

Participation in Business–Society Programs through
Continuing Education
(in percent)

Position	Involvement		
	None	Limited	Major
Liberal arts dean	30	52	19
Business school dean	37	55	8
University placement director	12	71	16
Business personnel director	25	52	23

Chi square value = 15.3
Degrees of freedom = 6
Significance level = .01

Note: Because of rounding, percentages may not total 100.

TABLE 5.25

Present Involvement with Special Minors and Programs Integrated
into Majors, Business and Liberal Arts
(in percent)

Position	Involvement		
	None	Limited	Major
Liberal arts dean	24	39	37
Business school dean	19	51	30

Chi square value = 2.3
Degrees of freedom = 2
Significance level = not significant

TABLE 5.26

Present Involvement with Exchange of Students through Electives
and Advisement, Business and Liberal Arts
(in percent)

Position	Involvement		
	None	Limited	Major
Liberal arts dean	14	40	46
Business school dean	8	67	25

Chi square value = 9.9
Degrees of freedom = 2
Significance level = .01

TABLE 5.27

Present Involvement with Exchange of Faculty and Team-Teaching
Programs, Business and Liberal Arts
(in percent)

Position	Involvement		
	None	Limited	Major
Liberal arts dean	44	51	4
Business school dean	48	49	3

Chi square value = 0.22
Degrees of freedom = 2
Significance level = not significant

among respondents from business schools and university placement
offices. However, significant involvement levels were also documented among liberal arts deans (especially for programs spon-
sored by the college or university).

Apparently universities are taking the lead over business and
government in sponsoring seminars and workshops as a means of
bringing business and the university together. The reasonably high
level of seminar participation by liberal arts schools to some extent
belies their characterization as being isolated from the real world
of business.

Likewise, roughly three-fourths of all liberal arts deans responding assessed their school's level of involvement with continuing-
education programs in areas such as management development, career preparation, and business-society relations as either limited
or major (see Tables 5.22 through 5.24). This again suggests that
liberal arts students do have access to vocationally oriented programs, at least upon graduation.

Levels of involvement with joint programs between liberal
arts and business schools—such as formally established minors in
each other's schools or informal exchanges of students through advisement and use of electives—were found to be higher than expected,

with nearly 80 percent or more of deans surveyed indicating either limited or major involvement in such programs (see Table 5.25 and 5.26). However, the degree of actual faculty exchange or use of team teaching across schools was found to be nearly nonexistent (see Table 5.27).

Apparently, the present view on most campuses is that student exposure to business or liberal arts subject matters is desirable, as reflected by curricula choices, but the degree of subject matter integration that would likely be produced by team teaching across the two disciplines is either infeasible or unnecessary.

Relative Career-Attractiveness of
Different College Majors

The profiles in Figure 5.2 present a rather interesting comparison of views regarding the desirability of different undergraduate educational backgrounds for college graduates entering business and industry. Significant differences (.01 level) were found among all four groups, with views of liberal arts deans diverging widely from those of the other three respondent groups.

While liberal arts deans saw little difference in the desirabilities of different backgrounds, among the other three respondent groups science and engineering (closely followed by business) were perceived to be the most suitable preparation for careers in business and industry.

A business minor with a liberal arts major was seen as more desirable than just a liberal arts background by all except liberal arts deans. Interestingly, the inclusion of a liberal arts minor to a business background had no effect on increasing the rated desirability of a business background—again, except among liberal arts deans. This latter finding would appear to be inconsistent with the general agreement among all groups that entry-level employees lack important communication and other interpersonal skills (the typical by-product of a liberal education). Apparently, corporations are espousing one set of requirements, while recruiting, based on a different set of criteria that emphasize technical specialization. This explanation echoes the criticisms leveled at business by William H. Whyte nearly 30 years ago. However, this apparent inconsistency might alternatively be explained by suggesting that while businessmen seek applicants with well-honed interpersonal skills, the business respondents in the survey were unconvinced that a liberal arts education could deliver them.

FIGURE 5.2

Desirability of Educational Background for Business and Industry

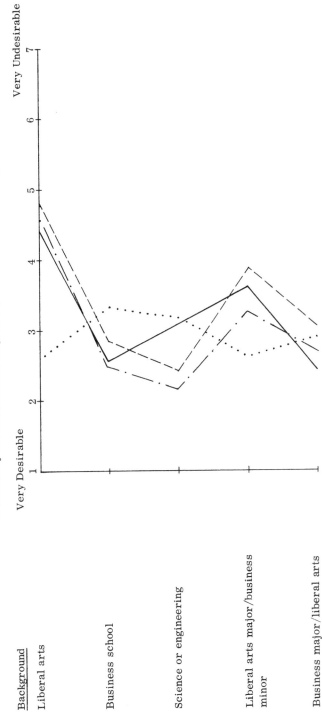

Code: ····· = liberal arts deans, ——— = business school deans, —·—·— = university placement directors, — — — = corporate personnel directors.

Differing Political and Economic Views

A comparison of the political and economic attitudes of deans and personnel directors is presented in Table 5.28. Significant attitudinal differences existed on nearly all issues presented. In most instances business school deans' attitudes were somewhat close to—but more moderate than—those of business personnel directors. Attitudes of university placement directors and liberal arts deans, respectively, showed increasing deviations from the attitudes of business deans and business personnel directors.

These differing attitudes shed some additional light on the difficulty of bridging the gap between university administrators and those in the business world. As long as basic attitudinal differences on such issues as these exist, it should not be surprising to see university curricula offerings deviate considerably from the career preparation desired by business.

Attitudes regarding specific relationships between business and government are summarized in Table 5.29. The attitudes of business school deans and corporate personnel directors are shown to be closer than the others. For a number of the statements, however, no significant attitudinal differences were found.

Table 5.30 presents a picture of the perceived influence of various groups on public policy. Two points of interest should be noted. First, the perceptions of all four respondent groups were not significantly different for the majority of questions asked. Second, the perceived power of groups such as corporate executives and top-level civil servants is seen as being very high (next to that of the president and Congress).

Finally, Table 5.31 presents a performance appraisal of U.S. business for each of the four groups. Interestingly, these appraisals do not vary in many regards. Significant differences were found, however, in areas such as providing safe products, maintaining strong competition, developing new products, and honesty in promotion of products. As might be expected on these issues, the views of business personnel directors were most closely paralleled by those of business school deans. These areas challenge business to more effectively communicate to others the efforts presently being made in new product development and the difficulties inherent in bringing new products to market.

TABLE 5.28

A Comparison of Political and Economic Attitudes
(in mean values)

Issue Posed	Liberal Arts Dean	Business School Dean	University Placement Director	Business Personnel Director	Significance Level
Generally speaking, our political system is working well in handling America's problems	3.9	3.9	3.8	4.4	n.s.
Competition is better than government regulation to make sure that the public gets what it pays for	3.0	2.3	2.9	2.2	.01
Rigorous application of wage and price controls is necessary to combat current inflation in the United States	4.3	5.3	4.3	5.0	.05
Leaders of the major institutions have lost confidence in their ability to control the direction in which the United States is moving	3.5	3.2	4.1	3.8	n.s.
Large companies have a major influence on the government agencies regulating them	2.3	3.1	2.7	3.6	.01
Differences in income between people in the United States should be reduced	4.2	5.0	4.8	5.5	.01
The federal government should support the creation of jobs in the public sector for those to whom the private sector does not provide employment	3.6	4.4	4.7	5.2	.01
Business should be required to have public members on boards of directors	4.3	4.2	4.8	5.3	.01
Meaningful social change cannot be achieved through traditional U.S. politics	4.8	5.3	5.1	4.6	.01
In times of recession, government spending should be held down to avoid a deficit	4.0	4.7	3.8	3.4	.01
Monopoly is growing in the United States	2.9	4.1	3.3	3.8	.05
Big corporations should be taken out of private ownership and run in the public interest	5.4	6.5	5.0	6.3	.01
The political power of the poor should be increased by encouraging community organizations and participation in control of government programs	3.8	4.7	4.3	4.5	n.s.
Government regulation is needed to maintain safe working conditions	2.6	3.4	3.2	3.7	.05

n.s. = not significant

Note: Mean values based on seven-point scale: 1 = strong agreement, 7 = strong disagreement.

TABLE 5.29

A Comparison of Views concerning the Proper Relationship between Business and Government
(in mean values)

Issue Posed	Liberal Arts Dean	Business School Dean	University Placement Director	Business Personnel Director	Significance Level
Workers should have a larger role in management of the plant in which they work	4.1	4.5	4.3	4.4	n.s.
The more government regulation, the less efficiently companies can operate	2.7	2.6	3.0	2.1	.01
The belief that "where special problems exist governmental solutions should be sought" has attained too high a measure of acceptance	2.9	2.2	2.5	2.3	n.s.
Special tax exemptions like the oil depletion allowance should be eliminated	3.6	4.2	3.7	3.8	n.s.
Poverty in the United States is now due mainly to cultural and psychological problems of the poor	4.4	4.5	4.6	4.1	n.s.
Costs to taxpayers of regulating business are well worth it	4.3	5.4	4.9	5.4	.01
Much higher inheritance taxes should be imposed to minimize the passing on of large family fortunes	5.0	5.0	5.3	5.6	n.s.
Business should be required to publish more information on profits	3.1	3.5	3.2	4.0	.01
The government should set a limit on the amount of profit any company can make	5.1	6.5	6.1	6.3	.01
Government regulation is the best way to ensure safe products	3.7	4.7	4.4	4.8	.01
Inflation is primarily caused by business	4.0	4.9	4.3	4.8	n.s.
Inflation is primarily caused by government	2.8	2.5	3.0	2.3	n.s.
Inflation is primarily caused by labor unions	3.4	3.6	3.3	3.1	n.s.
Inflation is primarily caused by consumers	4.2	4.3	4.1	4.4	.05

n.s. = not significant

Note: Mean values based on seven-point scale: 1 = strong agreement, 7 = strong disagreement.

DISCUSSION OF FINDINGS

What emerges from this study is a picture characterized by significant variations in perceptions and expectations concerning the appropriate educational training and background for business careers as well as concerning the performance of U. S. business and business education.

Both business school deans and deans of liberal arts perceived that schools and industry have separate roles to play in career preparation and training. In addition, they perceived present curricula programs as sufficient in preparing students for such careers. Interestingly, it is in these two areas where the perceptions of corporate personnel directors and academic deans are most divergent. These differences in perceptions pose a major barrier to closing the gap between university-program output and the career preparation desired by industry.

Given these differential perceptions, what are the implications for business education in the 1980s? The logical reaction might be to focus on the corporate personnel directors' recent calls for broader perspectives in educational training found here and elsewhere. [7] However, a closer examination of actual hiring criteria suggests quite a different thrust in preparing students for business careers. Industry's stated preference for graduates with science or engineering backgrounds over business (and especially liberal arts) backgrounds indicates that technical competence is weighted more heavily in hiring decisions than is a broader liberal arts perspective.

The maturing business disciplines face an important dilemma. Most functional business areas are at a point in their evolution where educators have a choice of either focusing on increasing technical competence within the discipline or emphasizing the development of generalists (developing interpersonal and communication skills along with a broader societal perspective). While increased specialization has been the major thrust in business education over the past decade, currently many (including the American Assembly of Collegiate Schools of Business) are calling for a shift to the broader societal view for the future. Is this shift in orientation desirable?

Based on the responses of the deans surveyed, the answer is likely to be yes. From an examination of corporate personnel directors' responses, the answer is less obvious. While they also express support for a broader orientation in training for careers in business, their actual selection preferences reflect a strong desire for technical competence. Analogous to many situations found in consumer goods marketing, the producer (in this case, the business

TABLE 5.30

A Comparison of Perceived Influence of Various Groups on Public Policy
(in mean values)

Influencing Group	Liberal Arts Dean	Business School Dean	University Placement Director	Business Personnel Director	Significance Level
Executives of large corporations	2.2	3.2	2.4	3.1	.01
High-level federal civil servants	2.4	2.3	2.9	2.5	n.s.
Intellectuals (university professors, social scientists, leading writers)	3.9	3.7	4.0	3.7	n.s.
Labor union leaders	2.4	2.8	2.4	2.5	n.s.
Major newspapers	2.6	2.6	2.6	2.5	n.s.
Members of Congress	2.2	1.9	2.1	2.3	n.s.
Military leaders (and the Pentagon)	2.9	3.6	3.0	3.4	n.s.
News magazines	3.1	3.4	3.0	3.4	n.s.
Consumer groups	3.8	3.7	3.4	3.5	n.s.
Political party leaders	2.8	2.6	2.6	2.7	n.s.
The president and White House staff	1.9	1.8	2.2	2.0	n.s.
Television news departments	2.8	2.6	2.4	2.8	.05
Very wealthy individuals and families	3.3	4.1	3.1	3.6	.05

n.s. = not significant

Note: Mean values based on seven-point scale: 1 = very high impact, 7 = very low impact.

TABLE 5.31

A Comparison of Perceptions regarding the Performance of U.S. Business

(in mean values)

Business Activity	Liberal Arts Dean	Business School Dean	University Placement Director	Business Personnel Director	Significance Level
Providing products and services that meet people's needs	2.4	1.9	2.1	2.1	n.s.
Producing safe products	3.0	2.5	3.1	2.8	.05
Improving the standard of living	2.6	2.0	2.2	2.2	n.s.
Maintaining strong competition	3.7	3.2	3.4	2.8	.01
Dealing with environmental problems	4.3	3.8	4.1	3.9	n.s.
Developing new products	2.3	2.5	2.3	2.6	.05
Being honest in what they say about their products	4.6	4.1	4.6	4.1	.05
Helping solve social problems	4.6	4.1	4.6	4.4	n.s.
Communicating with					
Employees	3.6	3.6	3.8	3.9	n.s.
Stockholders	2.8	2.9	3.0	3.0	n.s.
Customers	3.9	3.6	3.7	3.5	n.s.
General public	4.3	4.6	4.3	4.1	n.s.

n.s. = not significant

Note: Mean values based on seven-point scale: 1 = business doing a good job, 7 = business doing a poor job.

school) must attend to both what the customer (business) says as well as does. This research suggests the prime need is to increase technical competence within the various business functional areas.

A prerequisite to developing greater technical competence is to continue along the path of developing each functional area of business into a science. Given an increasingly rigorous and scientific foundation, an orientation toward technical specialization and competence does not necessarily imply vocationalism in its traditional sense but, rather, the evolution of the various business disciplines to the status of true professions.

NOTES

1. Chronicle of Higher Education, May 7, 1979, pp. 19-20.

2. Paul S. Hugstad and William E. Bell, "Curriculum Adaptation: A Model and Case," in Marketing: The Challenges and Opportunities, ed. Edward M. Mazze (Chicago: American Marketing Association, 1975); "MBA Recipients, Once Eagerly Sought, Now Eagerly Seek Jobs in Tight Market," Wall Street Journal, November 2, 1979.

3. Paul S. Hugstad and Robert M. Barath, "Bridging the Business School-Industry Gap: A Methodology for Aligning Graduate Marketing Programs with Industry Career Path Needs," in Marketing: 1776-1976 and Beyond, ed. Kenneth Bernhart (Chicago: American Marketing Association, 1976); "A Plan to Rate B-Schools by Testing Students," Business Week, November 19, 1979, pp. 171-74.

4. "Once Eagerly Sought," p. 171.

5. Dick W. Twedt, "Grant More Degrees, but Marketing Not Gaining Share," Marketing News, July 27, 1979, p. 28.

6. Hugstad and Barath, "Bridging the Gap."

7. Ibid.

6

MATURING
OF THE
BUSINESS SCHOOL

RESOLVING SOME OF THE ISSUES

How Much Specialization Is Desirable
at the Undergraduate and Graduate Levels?

While much of industry bemoans the lack of generalist skills
among its new employees, it continues to select entry-level job
applicants largely on the basis of their technical specializations.
This emphasis has not gone unnoticed by either university students
or university administrators.

While many deans (business as well as liberal arts) would prefer to moderate the trend toward curricula specialization, pressures
from business faculty (increasingly specialized themselves) and students (seeking an edge in today's highly competitive job markets)
have resulted in yet further calls for career-oriented, highly specialized programs.

While the recent popularity of graduate business programs
may appear to be in line with the trends in many areas toward
greater specialization, graduate business training, up until the
present, has been somewhat unique from other types of graduate
work.

The graduate school of business administration is not a
simple extension of the undergraduate school as can be
said of the graduate schools of other undergraduate colleges. In the latter cases, the extension consists of increased specialization where the undergraduate courses

are truly prerequisite to the graduate study. In the
case of business administration, however, the graduate
school tends to emphasize increased integration and gen-
eralization, which are essential characteristics of decision making by management. In this respect, the graduate school of business administration tends to become
more liberal while the other graduate schools tend to become more professional. [1]

The conflict between liberal and specialized orientations in the future may prove to be even greater.

How Does a Liberal Education Fit
into the New Vocationalism?

Both on and off campus, many continue to attack university
curricula for not providing enough exposure in the liberal arts; in
fact, what they are lamenting is the erosion of student competence
in skill areas such as oral and written communication, analytical
thinking, and interpersonal development. Since such skills were
historically the by-product of a good liberal arts education, many
have called for the reinstatement of more liberal arts courses in
business school curricula.

However, just as any subject matter can be taught liberally,
so can communication skills and analytical abilities be sharpened
outside the context of a liberal arts curriculum. Indeed, if these
skills alone were considered the only valuable by-product of liberal
arts programs, they might be more efficiently developed elsewhere
on campus (speech communication, business writing, or management science as examples). The recent trend toward offering business writing courses within the curriculum of the business school
may be interpreted as an attempt to more efficiently provide business students with liberal arts "skills."

What on the surface appears to be a call for liberalism by
business may in fact really be a call for increased basic skill competency.

Can Universities Teach the Skills
Business Is Demanding?

A corollary issue concerns whether or not a university is an appropriate—or the most effective—place to teach certain skills desired by business. It has been argued, for example, that universities are not well situated either in terms of physical constraints or, more important, psychological barriers to teach students about the "real world of business." Lacking both the latest in business equipment and staffed primarily with faculty devoid of significant managerial experience, universities have been criticized for even attempting to provide on-the-job type experiences for their students.

> An additional consideration is that most business school faculty members are poorly equipped to teach specific trade skills, since they have never themselves performed such tasks. The vast majority of American business school faculty members come from purely academic backgrounds. Most have gone straight from highly conceptual Ph.D. programs directly into teaching. They therefore tend to feel uncomfortable in vocational courses and usually attempt to subvert the nature of such courses by making them highly conceptual. This frustrates students as well as professors since, no matter what the catalog description says, the students come to a retailing class actually expecting to learn how to run a store, whereas the professor is constantly looking for an opportunity to deliver his favorite conceptual lecture.[2]

Cooperative education and internship programs have been regarded as the most realistic mechanisms for providing "real-world" experience. To the extent that business schools continue to evolve into professional schools, they may find the medical school model insightful for establishing more systematic and rigorous internship requirements.

BUSINESS SCHOOL TRENDS OF THE 1980s

Market Saturation for Business Graduates

Signs of market saturation levels being reached (especially for M.B.A.'s) have been noted over recent years.[3] This saturation has been due partly to the tremendous growth in the number of degrees awarded by business schools (cited earlier) and partly to a general disillusionment with the product of many of these programs. Enrollments of the ten largest undergraduate, M.B.A., and doctoral business programs are shown in Tables 6.1-6.3.

While some dissatisfaction has been expressed with technical or, more commonly, general business competence, much of the criticism stems from what employers perceive to be unreasonable expectations concerning early job responsibilities and rapid career advancement. Coupled with high initial salary demands and a view toward managing their own careers—not the company's business— M.B.A.'s have clearly fallen out of favor with many employers.

Current recessionary pressures have exacerbated these trends to the point where even some graduates from the top ten business schools are finding job hunting serious business.[4]

Development of a Three-Tiered Structure

Current market forces, combined with technology's persistent pressure toward increased function specialization, have resulted in the emergence of a three-tiered structure for business schools.

The top tier of business schools will likely remain essentially as they are, catering primarily to the needs of the Fortune 500 by training future top executives. Of the nearly five hundred business graduate programs in existence, as few as ten to twenty (most of them private) will continue in this role.* These schools will continue to disclaim undergraduate education in favor of high quality, liberal arts-laced professional orientations.

---

*AACSB accreditation figures showed that in 1977 only 19 percent of more than 1,100 undergraduate business programs were accredited. Of the 496 graduate business programs in place by 1979, only 27 percent were accredited.

TABLE 6.1

Ten Largest Undergraduate Programs in Business Based on 1981 Enrollments of Full-time and Total Students

Institution	Full-Time Students	Institution	Total Students
University of Texas at Austin	9,945	Bernard Baruch College, CUNY	10,837
Bernard Baruch College, CUNY	7,612	University of Texas at Austin	9,945
San Diego State University	7,230	Arizona State University	8,931
Arizona State University	6,776	San Diego State University	7,230
Texas A&M University	5,300	Drexel University	6,388
Western Michigan University	5,120	University of Texas at Arlington	6,210
University of South Florida	5,050	California State University, Long Beach	5,914
Northern Illinois University	4,952	Florida State University	5,548
Florida State University	4,827	Miami University	5,493
Miami University	4,806	Georgia State University	5,466

Source: Reprinted from AACSB Newsline 12, no. 3 (February 1982): 3, with permission of the American Assembly of Collegiate Schools of Business.

TABLE 6.2

Ten Largest Master's Programs in Business Based on 1981 Enrollments of Full-time and Total Students

Institution	Full-Time Students	Institution	Total Students
New York University	2,230	New York University	4,460
Harvard University	1,550	Georgia State University	2,444
University of Pennsylvania	1,385	Pepperdine University	2,400
Pepperdine University	1,300	Bernard Baruch College, CUNY	2,191
Georgia State University	1,143	University of Chicago	2,127
University of Chicago	1,134	Xavier University	1,962
University of Santa Clara	1,134	Adelphi University	1,900
Arizona State University	1,014	University of Houston	1,797
Columbia University	960	St. John's University	1,782
University of Texas at Austin	949	Temple University	1,729

Source: Reprinted from AACSB Newsline 12, no. 3 (February 1982): 3, with permission of the American Assembly of Collegiate Schools of Business.

TABLE 6.3

Ten Largest Doctoral Programs in Business Based on 1981 Enrollments of Full-time and Total Students

Institution	Full-Time Students	Institution	Total Students
University of Pennsylvania	239	University of Pennsylvania	239
University of Illinois–Champaign	225	University of Illinois–Champaign	229
University of Texas at Austin	146	Georgia State University	153
Michigan State University	140	University of Texas at Austin	146
University of California, Los Angeles	122	Michigan State University	140
Ohio State University	115	University of Arkansas	135
University of South Carolina	111	George Washington University	130
Indiana University	111	University of California, Los Angeles	122
University of Arkansas	106	Ohio State University	115
University of Chicago	90	Indiana University	115
University of Houston	90		
Louisiana State University	90		

Source: Reprinted from AACSB Newsline 12, no. 3 (February 1982): 3; with permission of the American Assembly of Collegiate Schools of Business.

101

Perhaps unintentionally, the apostles of vocationalism may also intensify class distinctions in higher education. It is unlikely that the most prestigious schools will commit themselves to vocationalism to any significant degree; a general education will continue to be the hallmark of the most privileged students. The greatest demand for vocational training and the greatest response is likely to be in the community colleges, the state schools and lesser private schools struggling to survive. There may come a division between academic and vocational institutions at the highest level comparable to that which has long existed at the secondary level. [5]

A second-level tier of business schools is presently evolving, primarily among the better-known public universities and selected private universities, which have developed extensively specialized graduate business programs. In some of these schools Master's of Science programs in functional areas such as accounting, finance, marketing, and so forth, have arisen to challenge the conventional supremacy of the M.B.A.

In addition, functional specialization has been combined with industry specialization to create hybrid programs, such as Marketing of the Arts, Health Care Marketing, and the like. Graduate-level specialties such as these have arisen at these universities in part as positioning strategies aimed at countering the prestige of the top-tier schools with greater marketplace application.

However, a good deal of the impetus for this specialization has come from the nature of these universities themselves. Because the faculties are typically large (fueled by large undergraduate enrollments), departmental staff tend to be highly specialized and the development of specialized curricula reflect a faculty desire to teach within their own specialties as much as a concern over marketplace requirements.

Currently, graduates of these specialized programs are enjoying marked success in securing initial employment within their specialties. It remains to be seen if this high level of market segmentation will prove attractive into the future as these graduates move up their career ladders and as traditional M.B.A.'s begin to compete more directly with them across presently less developed areas of business application (such as the nonprofit sector).

The third tier of business schools, comprised of the remaining 75 percent of business programs, will be markedly undergraduate in orientation while remaining heterogeneous with regard to quality and curricula. This tier will include most of the state universities and smaller, private and religiously affiliated colleges. Presently, a number of the larger state universities in this category have undergraduate enrollments in business in excess of 5,000 students. Their M.B.A. programs are usually of moderate size and are clearly ancillary to their undergraduate focus.

Many of these large undergraduate universities are fully accredited by the AACSB (at both levels) and provide extensive career-oriented specialization for their students. Their curricula are primarily focused on providing sound entry-level skills in the traditional, departmentalized mode. Furthermore, their programs tend to have a distinctly local, or at best regional, orientation—in many cases utilizing cooperative-type programs to build specific links to industry job markets.

Many of the lesser schools within this third tier were begun or enlarged primarily in response to enrollment losses elsewhere on campus, and they possess neither the quality of faculty nor curricula specialization to compete effectively with tier-two schools over the decade of the 1980s.

A substantial number of these business programs will likely become victims of a consolidation of business schools over the remainder of the decade. Others will survive by identifying a specific mission and tying themselves increasingly closer to their local business communities.

The business schools in these three tiers are not pure forms, and while business schools have long served different markets, the degree to which the public and business become aware of this three-tier typology will accelerate. This heightened awareness of strata will in turn crystallize the positions of existing business schools and lead to a concomitant need for yet further "nichemanship" and positioning.

Business School Faculty Crisis

As was the case during previous rapid growth periods, business schools are currently facing staffing problems of the first magnitude. Student enrollments have far outstripped most schools' abilities to add terminally qualified staff. While such a situation would normally bid up the value of new doctorates, the inability of business schools to separate their salary schedules from other

TABLE 6.4

Doctoral Degrees Awarded

Year	Graduates in All Disciplines	Business Graduates	Percentage of Business Graduates
1962	11,622	223	1.6
1965	16,467	321	2.0
1968	23,091	442	1.9
1971	32,113	810	2.5
1974	33,826	983	2.8
1977	33,244	869	2.6
1978	32,131	867	2.7
1979	32,756	863	2.6
1980	32,758	800	2.4

Source: Reprinted from National Center for Education Statistics, "Earned Degrees Conferred," AACSB Newsline 12, no. 1 (October 1981): 3, with permission of the American Assembly of Collegiate Schools of Business.

components of the university (as is common in medicine and law) has instead resulted in a continual decline in the output of business doctoral programs over the last five years (see Table 6.4). As shown in Table 6.5, at current doctoral output levels and given estimates of current and future staffing needs, it would take 6.7 years of production to fill existing staff vacancies and an additional 4.1 years of production to accommodate forecasted enrollment growth.

While a limited number of business schools have successfully lobbied for higher salary schedules (the University of California system, for example), the political ramifications on campus of

TABLE 6.5

Doctoral Supply and Demand by Business Schools: Average Annual Production and Consumption, 1976–80

Program	Net Gain of Doctorates[a]	Unfilled for 1980/81[b]	Planned Growth 1981/82[c]	Years of Production to Fill 1980/81 Vacancies[d]	Additional Years of Production to Fill 1981/82 Growth[e]
Accounting	23	511	262	22.2	11.4
Finance	30	267	145	8.9	4.8
Marketing	38	293	183	7.7	4.8
Economics	42	136	111	3.2	2.6
Operations research/decision sciences	38	117	83	3.1	2.2
Management	31	239	145	7.7	4.7
Management information systems	35	163	118	4.7	3.4
Industrial relations	15	33	32	2.2	2.1
Business policy/corporation strategy	18	80	58	4.4	3.2
Other	23	109	74	4.7	3.2
Total	292	1,948	1,211	6.7	4.1

aAdded doctorates minus number leaving academics.

bPositions for which schools sought doctorates.

cPositions for which schools have been authorized to seek doctorates.

dYears of necessary doctoral production to meet vacancies based on average 1976–80 net gain of doctorates.

eYears of necessary doctoral production to meet growth based on average 1976–80 net gain of doctorates.

Note: This table is based on survey responses from 48 doctoral producing and consuming schools and 269 consuming-only schools.

Source: Reprinted from "AACSB Task Force on Doctoral Supply and Demand," AACSB Newsline 11, no. 6 (August 1981): 3, with permission of the American Assembly of Collegiate Schools of Business.

TABLE 6.6

AACSB Salary Survey Data for Accredited Business Schools, 1970–80
(in thousands of dollars)

Academic Year	Dean	Professor	Associate Professor	Assistant Professor	Instructor
1970/71	28.0	18.4	15.3	13.2	9.5
1971/72	28.5	19.2	15.7	13.7	10.0
1972/73	30.9	20.3	16.6	14.2	11.0
1973/74	31.7	21.8	17.3	14.7	11.8
1974/75	n.a.	23.2	18.3	15.5	12.2
1975/76	31.7	24.8	19.3	16.4	12.6
1976/77	35.7	26.0	20.4	17.2	13.1
1977/78	39.0	27.9	21.9	18.3	14.6
1978/79	39.9	29.0	23.0	19.3	15.1
1979/80	44.9	31.7	24.8	21.0	16.5

n.a. = not available

Source: Reprinted from AACSB Newsline 12, no. 2 (December 1981): 1, with permission of the American Assembly of Collegiate Schools of Business.

TABLE 6.7

Mean Business Faculty Salaries by Discipline, 1981/82

(in thousands of dollars)

Discipline	Professor	Associate Professor	Assistant Professor	Instructor	New Doctorate
Accounting	37.1	29.8	24.9	19.6	27.7
Economics	36.2	27.4	23.1	18.1	22.7
Finance	37.6	29.8	26.0	19.9	26.5
Management	36.7	28.6	24.4	19.7	25.2
Marketing	36.5	29.4	24.4	18.7	26.1
Quantitative methods	37.0	28.9	24.4	18.6	25.8

Source: Reprinted from AACSB Newsline 12, no. 2 (December 1981): 3, with permission of the American Assembly of Collegiate Schools of Business.

107

creating yet another salary precedent for business schools, coupled with federal and state level funding constraints on universities, are portents of even greater problems ahead in attracting students into business doctoral programs.

Salary problems facing business school administrators are twofold. The failure of faculty salaries to keep up with the consumer price index (see Table 6.6) over the last decade has resulted in the loss of a number of senior business faculty to industry. This loss has in turn intensified pressure to hire new doctorates to service expanding enrollments. The result of the ensuing bidding war between business schools has been to drive up the price of new-hires beyond the salary range of many assistant professors already on staff. Table 6.7 illustrates the partial results of this "salary compression."

Given the lag in general salary levels for business school professors (resulting in declining real income) and the salary compression between ranks, perceived salary inequities have led to significant morale problems even for many of those professors choosing not to leave the university. While having less dramatic short-run effects on universities than the vacating of senior faculty positions, these morale problems may seriously jeopardize the quality of many business school programs over time.

As a result of these shortages, many business schools have become dangerously overreliant on part-time lecturers. This has in turn placed tremendous strain on meeting AACSB accreditation standards and has created pressures to modify existing standards to allow greater flexibility in applying staffing formulas. In response to member concerns, the AACSB is presently proposing adjustments to its accrediting criteria that would decrease the need for doctorally qualified business professors in meeting staffing needs by substituting teachers with Ph.D.'s in other disciplines or businessmen with extensive professional and scholarly credentials.[6]

Some business schools are choosing to restrict program enrollments and are making entrance requirements considerably more selective in order to further upgrade the quality of entering students. While many business school faculty applaud this shift to quality instead of quantity, such enrollment restrictions are being received on many campuses with mixed emotions. Since business schools were traditionally viewed as low-cost, high FTE generators ("cash cows" in business terminology), university administrators have typically resisted restricting business school enrollments, choosing instead to use such growth to subsidize other university programs that were either more costly or suffering enrollment declines.

TABLE 6.8

Average Salaries Offered 1980 Graduates with Bachelor's and
M.B.A. Degrees
(in dollars)

Discipline	Average Salary Offer
Bachelor's degree	
Humanities	12,888
General business	14,616
Economics	15,024
Accounting	15,516
Mathematics	17,700
Computer science	18,696
Electrical engineering	20,280
M.B.A. degree	
M.B.A. (nontechnical undergraduate)	21,540
M.B.A. (technical undergraduate)	23,652

Source: College Placement Council statistics, 1980.

Changing Student Population

Along with the spectacular growth of business school enrollments has come a shift in the composition and attitudes of the student body.

What we see now is a generation coming to college
that is as different from the baby boom as night and
day. Today's students are passive, conformist,
materialistic. . . . In the 60's students studied sociology so they could change the world; in the 70's
they studied psychology so they could change them-

TABLE 6.9

AACSB Business School Degrees, 1978/79

(in percent)

Academic Concentration	Bachelor's			M.B.A.		
	Male	Female	Percent of Total Degrees*	Male	Female	Percent of Total Degrees*
Accounting	30	32	30	11	13	12
Economics	3	2	3	2	1	2
Finance	10	7	9	14	14	14
Management	18	14	17	14	12	13
Marketing	16	19	17	6	9	7
Quantitative methods	1	1	1	2	2	2
Other	11	14	12	15	14	15
No formal concentration	11	11	11	37	34	36
Percent of total degrees	71	29		78	22	

*Because of rounding, percentages may not total 100.

Note: There were 26,242 M.B.A.'s granted and 85,176 Bachelor of Arts degrees awarded by AACSB schools.

Source: Compiled from AACSB office reports.

TABLE 6.10

Professional Degrees Awarded in 1980

Profession	Men	Women	Total
Business (M.B.A.)	47,117	12,382	59,499
Dentistry	4,802	719	5,521
Law	25,927	10,828	36,755
Medicine	11,523	3,523	15,046
Optometry	915	170	1,085
Theology	6,003	1,009	7,012
Veterinary medicine	1,233	602	1,835

Source: U.S., Department of Education, National Center for Education Statistics, Advanced Degrees Awarded, 1980.

selves; in the 80's they will study business administration so they can survive. [7]

Survival to many of today's young means more than just the promise of an entry-level job; it means a job that affords them the maintenance of their life-style expectations. The economic benefits of early specialization, shown in Table 6.8, have not gone unnoticed by today's students.

In recent years business schools have also begun to draw students from a much wider diversity of backgrounds. A key factor in the growth of business enrollments has been the increased matriculation of women. While women are still underrepresented in business schools, they have made substantial gains, accounting for 82 percent of all growth in undergraduate business degrees and 45 percent of total growth in graduate degrees between the years 1973 and 1980. [8] As shown in Table 6.9, female enrollments in the areas of accounting, marketing, and management are especially strong.

During this period significant numbers of students from across campus also began to apply for admission to business schools. With medical school and law school options already closed to most, the "new vocationalism" spirit pushed more and more high-caliber undergraduate students toward the newer professions, such as business. By 1980 graduate business degrees awarded had far outpaced other categories of professional degrees (see Table 6.10). At the graduate level, students from the sciences and engineering were being attracted to MBA programs as a means of moving around career hurdles in their chosen specialties. All of these changes can be viewed as positive signs of the maturing of business as a professional school.

NOTES

1. D. Sharon, "Objectives: Should They Be Different for Undergraduate and Graduate Level Instruction?" Collegiate News and Views 13 (October 1960): 8.

2. Bennett L. Rudolph, "Conceptualization vs. Vocationalism: Defining the Role of Marketing Education in a Liberal Arts Contest," Journal of Marketing Education, Fall 1981, p. 25.

3. "MBA Recipients, Once Eagerly Sought, Now Eagerly Seek Jobs in Tight Market," Wall Street Journal, November 2, 1979.

4. "The MBA Glut Is Now Hitting the Top Ten," Business Week, March 15, 1982, p. 30.

5. James Hitchcock, "The New Vocationalism," Change, April 1973, p. 50.

6. "Standards Changes Proposed," AACSB Newsline 12, no. 1 (April 1982): 1.

7. Landon Jones, "After the Baby Boom Generation: The Students of The 1980's," Chronicle of Higher Education vol. 24 (May 18, 1981).

8. AACSB Newsline 12, no. 1 (October 1981): 3.

7

FUTURE
OF THE
BUSINESS SCHOOL

It is somewhat ironic that business schools, presently at their
zenith in popularity, face a present and a future that are so fraught
with problems. During a time of immense success (judged by student enrollment pressures), many business schools can only be
characterized as in a state of mild disarray. Classroom facilities
are overcrowded, full-time faculty are in scarce supply, curricula
are often lagging behind recent industry advancements, and significant numbers of existing faculty are either planning to leave education or exhibiting signs of "faculty burnout" with an accompanying
lessening of their effectiveness.

The growth in popularity of business schools on many campuses has not brought with it the traditional benefits of increased
power, prestige, and resources; it has, instead, created a strained
production mentality whereby faculty and curricula are viewed in the
context of "pumping out" increased numbers of "widgets" to pay for
institutional overhead and alternative university programs. The
1980s represent a critical period in the evolution of the business
school, a period that will likely determine whether business is truly
elevated to the status of a profession (with full university honors
and privileges), or whether it returns to its previous status as
second-class citizen, a necessary evil on campus that must be carefully controlled and "milked."

Which of these scenarios comes closer to predicting the future
will largely depend on the reaction of three key groups: senior university administrators, business school administrators, and corporate executives.

Taking the position that while increasing the professional
school status of business may not be <u>pareto optimal</u>, it is likely

115

preferable to returning it to "serfdom," the following set of recommendations are offered to deal with its present plight.

Recommendation 1: The business community must become more directly involved in both shaping the role of the business school and in providing for its financial support.

Now is an especially opportune time for businesses to become directly involved with business schools in their respective communities. Involvement in areas such as curriculum change, development of truly effective internship programs, and the sharing of management development resources and ideas must be increased.

Financial support of business schools is needed not only in terms of supplemental funding for facilities and faculty salaries but also in areas such as donations of classroom-related equipment and executive teaching time. Indeed, one of the greatest opportunities presently is to more fully utilize key business personnel to help fill the aforementioned gap in teaching faculty. To this end, quasi-formal arrangements should be made for the continued exchange of faculty and executives between business schools and industry, to the mutual benefit of both parties.

Credential requirements for teaching in business schools likewise need reexamination. Present economic market forces are driving a wedge between those in education and those in business, forcing many business faculty to choose between economic survival (and prosperity) and their initially chosen role as educator. If current faculty quality is to be maintained and, more importantly, newer faculty attracted, hiring and retention criteria for all but the top-tier business schools will likely need to reflect greater emphasis on business success and applied business contribution rather than academic credentials (Ph.D.'s) and journal publications.

In the future, more attention must also be paid to faculty development. Pierson had this advice over 30 years ago:

> The direction a particular school takes is thus largely
> a matter of faculty development. Much more atten-
> tion needs to be paid than in the past to keeping each
> school's faculty growing. Sabbatical leaves, summer
> institutes, special seminars, research aids, and other
> devices need to be more fully utilized. A great deal of
> attention should be paid to assessing the strengths and
> weaknesses of a faculty and to recruiting new staff. An

over all plan of faculty development may prove helpful, but this is an area in which individual staff members must play a leading role.[1]

In general, the present crises faced by business schools are a significant incentive to close the existing gap between the business and the university communities through working together.

Recommendation 2: Business school deans and faculty must stop reacting and begin proacting to market shifts in student demand and funding.

Business schools must apply their own concepts (strategic planning, market segmentation, product-line management, and so forth) more effectively to their own situations. Specific missions, plans, and programs must be developed and implemented inside the unique context of their educational environments to more efficiently allocate increasingly scarce campus resources.

Business schools must resist being all things to all people. Demands by university administrators to "prop up" enrollment must be met with a well-thought-out rationale for alternatives, such as ensuring program quality and enrollment stability.

Likewise, industry's simultaneous demands for liberally educated employees with immediate job-related skills must be rationalized. Some of these demands could likely be fulfilled elsewhere on campus (liberal arts, communication department) and some through on-the-job training. Business schools must reaffirm their central role as one of developing decision-making skills and resist calls to provide vocational skills that are better developed elsewhere.

Such a viewpoint could help stabilize student enrollments across campus, remove some of the enrollment pressures on undergraduate business course enrollments, and position the business school as a prestige component of the university. The business school could then become a valuable bridge to the community, much as law and medical schools have.

If educators (both in the business school and across campus) and industry respond to the above challenges, the future of the business school looks bright indeed. Not only will it emerge from the 1980s as a more integral component of the university but its ties to business and the community will be greatly strengthened, to the mutual benefit of all.

Recommendation 3: Other senior university administrators must begin viewing business schools in a broader perspective, not as merely convenient short-run solutions to campus enrollment downturns and shortfalls in federal and state funding.

Much of the present dilemma facing business schools is rooted in their historical development as a stepchild to the liberal arts. As such, full-fledged adult acceptance on most campuses has been measured in small increments. At stake, of course, has been more than collegial prestige. University staffing and resource formulas are notoriously tied to program enrollment statistics (the now well-known "FTE game"). As such, the quantitative rise of the business school was viewed by many as more of a threat to budget power than to academic integrity.

While business schools' present growth and popularity among students have ameliorated some of the historical disdain, on most campuses the business school is still commonly referred to as trade tech or some other such pejorative phrase.

Senior campus administrators must begin to work together to build bridges between the business school and other campus entities (especially the liberal arts school) to the mutual benefit of all concerned.

A CONCLUDING COMMENT

The role of the business school in its brief 100-year history has evolved from the concept of a liberal education for men of privilege to today's concept of business education as a route to social mobility for men and women of all backgrounds and persuasions. Viewed today more as a meritocracy than as a social club, the business school has witnessed a concomitant increase in both its quantitative and qualitative growth.

While the pendulum has periodically swung back and forth over the years from liberalism to vocationalism and back again, presently the business school stands squarely between these poles, albeit being drawn increasingly again toward the profession. Far from being casual observers of these shifts, business executives, university administrators, and faculty have a great interest in the near-term direction taken by the business school. As business education continues to play a more central role in meeting societal challenges, it seems paramount that all groups concerned come together to ensure the continued maturation of the business school into a true professional school, modeled after those in medicine and law.

Pressures toward short-run vocational emphases must be resisted and replaced by an enduring commitment to high quality, broadly based educational programs. To do otherwise would be to further isolate the business school on campus, which in turn would eventually lead to disillusionment among many of its present supporters in the business community as well.

If the lessons of the past century of educational development are to be learned and the gains in maturity protected, business schools must continue to carefully balance the myriad of conflicting demands being placed on them, while simultaneously solving their present crises of funding and faculty staffing. To this end, more and better bridges must be built between the academy and business, and an honest and constructive dialogue must be stimulated to address the appropriate present and future roles of business education. It is hoped that the present discussion in some way contributes toward that end.

NOTE

1. Frank Pierson, The Education of American Businessmen (New York: McGraw-Hill, 1959), p. xv.

BIBLIOGRAPHY

THE DEVELOPMENT AND EVOLUTION OF
THE BUSINESS SCHOOL PRIOR TO 1950

Adams, James Truslow. "A Test for American Business." New
York Times Magazine, January 10, 1937, pp. 1-2, 27.

American Council on Education. Business Education at the College
Level. American Council on Education Studies, Series 1, Re-
ports of Committees of the Council, no. 7. Washington, D. C.:
The Council, 1939.

_____. "The Relationship between a College of Commerce and a
Liberal Arts Division." Proceedings of the 23rd Annual Meet-
ing, American Assembly of Collegiate Schools of Business,
May 1941, pp. 65-68.

_____. "The Survey of Schools of Business." Proceedings of the
22nd Annual Meeting, American Assembly of Collegiate
Schools of Business, April 1940, pp. 23-29.

Armstrong, J. Evan. "Training and Outlook in Business Vocation."
Junior College Journal, November 1936.

Aurner, Robert. "Business Communication Courses in the College
Business Administration Department." National Business
Education Quarterly 15 (December 1946): 31-44.

Baker, E. "Liberal Education and Industrial Management." Adult
Education, March 1946.

Beard, Miriam, A History of the Business Man. New York: Macmillan, 1938.

Bossard, James, and J. Frederic Dewhurst. University Education
for Business. Philadelphia: University of Pennsylvania
Press, 1935.

Browne, C. G. "Is Business Education Meeting Needs of Business?"
Journal of Business Education vol. 23 (April 1948).

Cambridge University Committee. University Education and Business. Cambridge: At the University Press, 1946.

Crosbaugh, Clyde J. "Objectives of Collegiate Business Education." Journal of Business Education 21 (February 1946): 16-18.

Dale, H. C. "The Responsibilities of Schools of Business Administration to Economic Statesmanship." Proceedings of the 19th Annual Meeting, American Assembly of Collegiate Schools of Business, March 1937, pp. 18-23.

Endicott, Frank S. "An Analysis of Factors Relating to the College Graduates in Business." U.S. Education Forum, May 1947, pp. 30-32.

_____. The Guidance and Counseling of Business Education Students. Cincinnati: South-Western, 1946.

Fries, Albert C. "College Training for Business." Journal of Business Education 20 (March 1945): 11-12.

Gilrett, H. "How Well Are the Liberal Arts Defended?" Business Education World, September 1946.

Griswold, A. W. "Liberal Education is Practical Education." New York Times Magazine, November 29, 1933, p. 13.

Hansen, Carl W. "Curriculum Practices on the University Level." American Business Education Association Yearbook 5 (1947): 211-16.

Haynes, Benjamin, and Harry Jackson. A History of Business Education in the United States. Cincinnati: South-Western, 1935.

Hofstadter, Richard, and C. Dewitt Hardy. Development and Scope of Higher Education in the U.S. New York: Columbia University Press, 1952.

Hutchinson, R. M. "Liberal vs. Practical Education." Rotarian 69 (September 1946): 14-15.

Irwin, L. B. "Education and the Businessman." Social Studies, vol. 40, February 1949.

Johnson, Emory R. The Wharton School—Its First Fifty Years.
    Philadelphia: University of Pennsylvania, Wharton School,
    1931.

Kerr, Clark. "The Schools of Business Administration." Annual
    Proceedings of the American Association of Collegiate Schools
    of Business, 1957.

Kimmel, W. G. "Some Possibilities for Closer Cooperation be-
    tween the Social Studies and Business Education." Journal of
    Business Education, vol. 8, 1935.

Knepper, Edwin G. A History of Business Education in the United
    States. Ann Arbor, Mich.: Edwards Brothers, 1941.

Lyon, Leverett S. Education for Business. Chicago: University of
    Chicago Press, 1931.

Marshall, Leon C. "School of Commerce." In Higher Education in
    America, edited by R. A. Kent. Boston: Ginn, 1930.

Matherly, Walter J. "The Relationship of the School of Business to
    the College of Liberal Arts." Proceedings of the 19th Annual
    Meeting, American Association of Collegiate Schools of Busi-
    ness, March 1937, pp. 5-17.

Natiens, L. J. "Business before Culture." North American Re-
    view 229 (June 1930): 705-13.

Nystrum, Paul H. "College Training and the New Deal." Proceed-
    ings of the 17th Annual Meeting, American Association of Col-
    legiate Schools of Business, April 1935, pp. 20-27.

Oliver, Robert T. "The Old Dilemma: Vocational Training or
    Liberal Arts?" School and Society 62 (October 1945): 219-20.

Olsen, H. V. The Collegiate Schools of Business in American Edu-
    cation. Third Annual Delta Pi Epsilon Lecture. Cincinnati:
    South-Western, 1944.

Prickett, A. L. Collegiate Schools of Business in American Educa-
    tion. Cincinnati: South-Western, 1945.

Puckett, Cecil. "Business Curriculum Practices on the College and University Level." American Business Education Association Yearbook 5 (1947): 217-25.

Rose, J. R. "Business Education in a University." Journal of Business, vol. 20 (October 1947).

Rubican, R. "Business Looks at Education." Journal of Business Education, vol. 23 (March 1948).

Simon, S. I. "Undergraduate Business Colleges Are Too Specialized." Journal of Business Education, vol. 24 (March 1949).

Spencer, William R. "The Plan of the Natural Sciences." Journal of Business 5 (October 1932): 52-55.

Stevenson, Russell A. "The Proposed Survey of Business Education." Proceedings of the American Assembly of Collegiate Schools of Business, April 1939, pp. 8-26.

Stuart, Henry W. Liberal and Vocational Studies in the College. Stanford, Calif.: Stanford University Press, 1918.

Veblen, Thorstein. The Higher Learning in America. New York: B. W. Huebsch, 1918.

Willits, Joseph H. "Business Schools and Training for Public Service." Proceedings of the American Assembly of Collegiate Schools of Business, April 1935, pp. 8-17.

BUSINESS EDUCATION UNDER ATTACK: THE 1950s

Aberle, Jr. "An Evaluation of a College's Curriculum in Business." National Business Education Quarterly 24 (October 1955): 1-8.

Allen, Louis A. "Do We Know What We're Looking For?" Personnel, vol. 37 (January-February 1960).

American Association of Collegiate Schools of Business. Views on Business Education. Chapel Hill: University of North Carolina Press, 1960.

"Are B-Schools on the Right Track?" Business Week, April 13,
1957, p. 50.

Austin, C. L. "What Industry Expects from Higher Education."
Association of American Colleges Bulletin, December 1953.

Bailey, Nathan A. "Education for Business Leadership." Collegiate News and Views 13 (March 1960): 15-16.

Baltzell, E. Digby. "Bell Telephone's Experiment in Education."
Harper's 210 (March 1955): 73-77.

Barry, F. Gordon, and C. G. Coleman, Jr. "Tougher Program for
Management Training." Harvard Business Review 36 (November-December 1958): 117-25.

Benninger, L. J. "Trends in the Development of Higher Education
for Business." American Business Education Association
Yearbook 15 (1957): 47-52.

Besse, Ralph M. "The Vision of the Future." Vital Speeches 28
(July 1957): 551-55.

Bienvenue, B. J. "Status of Schools of Business Administration in
a Changing Society." Southwestern Social Science Quarterly,
1960 Supplement, pp. 245-49.

Bolman, F. De W. "Romance between Colleges and Industry?"
Education Records 36 (April 1955): 150-56.

Booher, Edward E. "Does Business Need the Liberal Arts Graduate?" Think, April 1957.

Borland, Helen. "Collegiate Business Education Problems."
American Business Education 2 (May 1950): 215-20.

Bradley, Joseph F. "The Emergence of Business as a Profession."
Collegiate News and Views 11 (March 1958): 11-15.

Brickman, W. W. "Liberal Education and Industrial Leadership."
School and Society 85 (September 1957): 253-54.

Broehl, Wayne G. "Looking Around: Do Business and Religion Mix?" Harvard Business Review, March–April, 1958, pp. 139-52.

Brown, Courtney. "Business in Cap and Gown." Saturday Review, January 19, 1957, pp. 16-18.

_____. "Human Problems First." Saturday Review, November 21, 1953, pp. 3-6.

Brown, Francis J., ed. "Higher Education under Stress." Annals of the American Academy of Political and Social Science, vol. (September 1955).

Bryant, D. L. "Humanities: Basis for Business." Office Executive, vol. 33 (May 1958).

Butts, Freeman, and Lawrence Cremin. A History of Education in American Culture. New York: Holt, Rinehart and Winston, 1953.

Calkins, Robert D. "Liberal Arts in Business Training." Association of American Colleges Bulletin 38 (May 1952): 329-35.

Calvert, Robert, Jr. Career Patterns of Liberal Arts Graduates. Cranston, R. I.: Carroll Press, 1969.

Campbell, William R. "Integrating English in Professional Business Courses at the Undergraduate Level." Collegiate News and Views, vol. 9 (October 1956).

Carroll, Thomas H. "Business Education in the Next Quarter Century." Diary of Alpha Kappa Psi, Winter 1959, pp. 3-7.

_____. "Education for Business: A Dynamic Concept and Process." Accounting Review 33, no. 1 (January 1958): 4.

Carroll, Thomas H., ed. Business Education for Competence and Responsibility. Chapel Hill: University of North Carolina Press, 1954.

Clark, H. "Education in Our Complex Society." NEA Journal, April 1962, p. 52.

Clark, John J., and Blaise J. Opulente. "Challenge of Business Education." Redman, Winter 1959.

Cochran, Thomas C. Basic History of American Business. Princeton, N.J.: Amil Books, 1959.

Compton, Wilson. "Corporation Support." Annals of the American Academy of Political and Social Science 301 (September 1955): 140-47.

Copland, Melvin T. And Mark an Era. Boston: Little, Brown, 1958.

Corrigan, Francis. "Whither Collegiate Business Education?" School and Society 83 (February 1956): 45-47.

Curtice, H. H. "Industry and Education in a Free Society." Journal of Higher Education 26 (October 1955): 357-60.

Cutler, Howard. "Organization of Collegiate Schools of Business." Collegiate News and Views 7 (October 1953): 1-8.

Danskin, Donald R. "Education for Business in Church-Related Liberal Arts Colleges." Journal of Business Education 31 (April 1956): 319.

Davidson, Carther. "Spelling Out Specifics in Business-Liberal Arts Exchange: A College President's View." Association of American Colleges Bulletin 39 (December 1953): 565-71.

Davis, Keith. "Human Relations as a Basis." American Business Education Association Yearbook 14 (1957): 136-49.

Diebold, J. "Business Management in Transition." Systems 22, no. 1 (January 1959): 24-25.

Donovan, T. R. "Socioeconomic and Educational Factors Influencing the Achievement Level of Individuals in Large-scale Organizations." Sociology and Social Research 46 (July 1962): 416-25.

Dressel, Paul L., Lewis B. Mayhew, and Earl J. McGrath. The Liberal Arts as Viewed by Faculty Members in Professional

Schools. New York: Teachers College, Columbia University, 1959.

Drucker, Peter. "Graduate Business Schools." Fortune 42 (August 1950): 92-94.

_____. The Practice of Management. New York: Harper & Brothers, 1954.

Etier, F. "General Education, Its Relation to Business Education." Journal of Business Education, vol. 28 (May 1953).

Fielden, John S. "Thinking Ahead: Business Education." Harvard Business Review 37, no. 6 (November-December 1959): 35-42, 182-88.

Fries, Albert. "The Role of Collegiate Institutions in Stimulating Effective Leadership." National Business Education Quarterly 23 (May 1955): 31-33.

Giddens, Paul H. "Business and the Liberal Arts." Association of American Colleges Bulletin 39 (December 1953): 554-64.

Glos, R. E. "The Establishment of Curriculums in Higher Education for Business." American Business Education Association Yearbook 14 (1957): 153-63.

Goldwin, Robert, and Charles A. Nelson. "The Inhumane Businessman." In Toward the Liberally Educated Executive, edited by Robert Goldwin and Charles A. Nelson. White Plains, N.Y.: Fund for Adult Education, 1959.

_____. Toward the Liberally Educated Executive. New York: Fund for Adult Education, 1959.

Gordon, Robert A., and James E. Howell. Higher Education for Business. New York: Columbia University Press, 1959.

Greenewalt, C. H. "Education and U.S. Business: The Culture of the Businessman." Saturday Review, January 19, 1957, pp. 11-13.

Hamilton, Herbert A. "The Present Status of Higher Education for Business." American Business Education Association Yearbook 14 (1957): 30–46.

Hamilton, Roger S. "Business Administration Courses Adjusted to Community Needs." American Business Education 7 (May 1955): 281–83.

Havemann, Ernest, and Patricia West. They Went to College. New York: Harcourt, Brace, 1952.

Hazard, L. "Humanities for the Businessman." Harvard Business Review 38 (November 1960): 39–44.

Hofstadter, Richard, and C. DeWitt Hardy. The Development and Scope of Higher Education in the United States. New York: Columbia University Press, 1952.

Holman, Ross L. "Religion in Business." American Business, January 1955, p. 24.

"How to Be a Business Man." Economist, August 31, 1957, pp. 687–88.

Hughes, Eugene H. "The Need for Discovering the Fundamentals and Bases of Higher Education for Business." American Business Education Association Yearbook 14 (1957): 55–56.

Hurley, Morris E. "Liberal Arts as a Basis." American Business Education Association Yearbook 14 (1957): 67–68.

Hutchins, Robert. The Higher Learning in America. New Haven, Conn., 1936.

"Industry and College: Partners in Development." Steel 139 (November 1956): 119–26.

Katz, M. "Liberal Education in Education for Business." Business Horizons 2, no. 3 (Fall 1959): 80.

Kellenber, Elizabeth. "Business Education in the Liberal Arts College." Catholic Business Education Association, June 1958.

Kerr, Clark. "The Schools of Business Administration." Proceedings of the American Assembly of Collegiate Schools of Business, 1957.

Kirkland, Edward Chase. Dream and Thought in the Business Community 1860-1900. Ithaca, N.Y.: Cornell University Press, 1956.

Kirkpatrick, Forrest H. "Business Education in the Future." Diary of Alpha Kappa Psi, Summer 1958.

Kozelka, Richard. "Professional Education for Business Administration." Higher Education 9 (April 1953): 184.

Lee, Dorothy E. "Historical Development of Business Schools from Colonial Times." American Business Education Association Yearbook 14 (1957): 16-29.

"Liberal Education and Industrial Leadership." School and Society 85 (September 1957): 253.

Lockley, Lawrence C. "Business Education and the Humanities." School and Society 5 (December 1951): 417-20.

McCormick, J. P. "The English Major as a Business Man." College English 17 (May 1956): 486-87.

McGrath, E. J. "Education Profession and Public Affairs." Journal of Public Accountancy, April 1958.

_____. The Graduate School and the Decline of Liberal Education. New York: Teachers College, Columbia University.

McGrath, Earl J. Liberal Education in the Professions. New York: Teachers College, Columbia University, 1959.

McGrath, Earl J., and Charles H. Russell. Are Liberal Arts Colleges Becoming Professional Schools? New York: Teachers College, Columbia University, 1958.

Mackay, LaMar, and Donald Bacon. "Are the Business Schools Beneficial?" Wall Street Journal, March 17, 1958.

McPhelin, Michael. "The Humanities in Education for Business."
Collegiate News and Views 7 (October 1954): 1-6.

"Management Pattern: Some Trophies from the 'Jungle.'" Business Week, February 16, 1963, p. 140.

Marshall, L., ed. The Collegiate School of Business. Chicago: University of Chicago Press, 1928.

May, F. B. "Business Administration Curricula and the New Research Techniques." Southwestern Social Science Quarterly, 1959 Supplement, pp. 41-48.

Mee, John R. "Management Philosophy for Professional Executives."
Business Horizons 11 (1956): 5-11.

Mortimer, C. G. "Industry's Stake in Education." Vital Speeches 29 (February 1963): 270-73.

Mulcahy, Richard E. "Why a Business College?" American Review, January 11, 1958, pp. 421-24.

Murray, E. B. "Business Values of Classical Training." Classical Journal 52 (November 1956): 49-53.

Nelson, C. A. "Liberal Education for Public Service?" Public Administration Review 18 (Fall 1958): 278-89.

Nelson, Charles. "The Liberal Arts in Management." Harvard Business Review 37 (May-June 1959): 91-100.

"New Look in Business Schools—Stanford's B-School." Business Week, July 17, 1961, pp. 156-58.

Newcomer, James. "Liberal Arts in the Business Administration Curriculum." Liberal Education 45 (May 1959): 285-95.

Newcomer, Mabel. The Big Business Executive—The Factors That Made Him, 1900-1959. New York: Columbia University Press, 1955.

Nichols, B. J. "Education for Management Leadership." Vital Speeches 28 (December 1961): 154-57.

Nickerson, Albert L. "Climbing the Managerial Ladder." Saturday Review, November 21, 1953, pp. 38-39.

Nicks, Earl. "Problems of Business Educators in Collegiate Schools of Business." National Business Education Quarterly 20 (May 1952): 17-20.

Norton, K. B. "Latin Major in Industry." Classical Journal 52 (October 1956): 13-14.

Odiorne, G. S. "Uneasy Look at College Recruiting." Vital Speeches 28 (November 1961): 60-63.

Olson, Paul. "The Professional Economist and Economic Education." Collegiate News and Views 11 (March 1958): 1-6.

Pamp, Frederick E., Jr. "Liberal Arts as Training for Business." Harvard Business Review 33 (May-June 1955): 42-55.

Patterson, W. D. "Business: Our Newest Profession." Saturday Review, January 19, 1957, pp. 14-15.

Peck, C. E. "Qualities Employers Look For in a College Graduate." Collegiate News and Views 11 (December 1958): 13-16.

Peck, M. A. "Business Education in the Liberal Arts College." American Business Education, vol. 14 (December 1957).

Pierson, Frank C. The Education of American Businessmen. New York: McGraw-Hill, 1959.

"Popularity Swamps Business Schools." Business Week, December 15, 1956, pp. 193-94.

Prentis, H. W., Jr. "Liberal Education for Business and Industry." American Association of University Professors Bulletin, Autumn 1952.

Prime, John. "Collegiate Business Education in America." National Business Education Quarterly 21 (October 1953): 43-46.

"Problems of Business Education." Journal of Business 34 (January 1961): 1-9.

Randall, Clarence M. A Business Man Looks at Liberal Education. White Plains, N. Y.: Adult Education Association, 1956.

Robinson, Marshall A. "The Academic Content of Business Education." Journal of Higher Education 33 (March 1962): 131-40.

Sarah, Sister M. "The Liberal Arts vs. Specialized Education." Journal of Business Education 35 (May 1960): 350-51.

Schovill, H. T. 50 Years of Education for Business at the University of Illinois. Urbana: University of Illinois Press, 1952.

Shepherd, David A. Liberal Education in an Industrial Society. Public Affairs Pamphlet no. 248. New York: Public Affairs Committee, 1957.

_____. "Management in Search of Men." Atlantic Monthly 197 (March 1956): 65-66.

"Should a Business Man Be Educated?" Fortune 45 (April 1953): 113-14.

Siegle, Peter E. New Direction in Liberal Education for Executives. New York: Center for the Study of Liberal Education for Adults, 1958.

Silk, Leonard S. The Education of Businessmen. New York: Committee for Economic Development, 1960.

Spengler, Joseph. "An Economist Views Collegiate Business Education." Collegiate News and Views 8 (March 1955): 1-3.

Stout, Edward. "University Training for Business." Collegiate News and Views 10 (December 1956): 9-12.

Taylor, Weldon. "Are Business Schools Meeting the Challenge?" Collegiate News and Views 10 (October 1956): 1-6.

Terry, George. "Adjusting the College Curriculum to Demands of the Business Office." American Business Education 8 (October 1951): 23-26.

Thompson, Willard. "Critics Challenge College Business Programs." California Business Education Association Bulletin, vol. 18 (May 1960).

Tidwell, M. Fred. "The Graduate Business School of Tomorrow." American Business Education 7 (March 1951): 212-16.

Tonne, Herbert A. "How Liberal Are the Liberal Arts?" Journal of Business Education 35 (March 1960): 248.

Trace, Arthur S. "The Liberal Arts: Detractors and Defenders." Modern Age, Fall 1959.

U. S., Department of Health, Education and Welfare, Office of Education. Education for the Professions, edited by Lloyd E. Blauch. Washington, D. C.: Government Printing Office, 1955.

Weimer, Arthur N. "Business and General Education." Business Horizons 32 (June 1957): 1-6.

Wharton Survey Advisory Committee. A Program for the Wharton School. Philadelphia: University of Pennsylvania, 1957.

"What Future Executives Must Know." Nation's Business 44 (August 1956): 34.

White, A. L. "Closer Cooperation between Business and Education." Dun's Review, June 1951.

Whitehead, Alfred North. "Introduction: On Foresight." Business Adrift. New York: W. B. Donham, 1931.

Whitmore, E. W. "Economics in the Curricula of Schools of Business." American Economic Review 46, no. 2 (May 1956): 554.

_____. "Too Many Specialists—Not Enough Top Executives." American Business 22, no. 8 (August 1952): 16.

Whyte, William H., Jr. "The New Illiteracy." Saturday Review, November 21, 1953, pp. 33-35.

_____. The Organization Man. New York: Doubleday, 1956.

Williams, Lloyd P. "The Educational Consequences of Laissez-Faire." School and Society 85 (February 1957): 38-39.

Wingate, John W. "The Question of Business Specialization in Colleges and Universities." Collegiate News and Views 13 (May 1960): 1-6.

THE MATURING OF THE BUSINESS
SCHOOL: THE 1960s

American Assembly of Collegiate Schools of Business: Views on Business Education. Chapel Hill: University of North Carolina Press, 1960.

Bangs, F. Kendrick. "Curriculum Revision in Business Education at the Collegiate Level." National Business Education Quarterly 28 (May 1960): 13-17.

Bowen, H. "Business Schools and the University—Opportunities Reform." In Entrepreneurship and the Dynamics of the Educational Process, edited by C. C. Ling. St. Louis: American Assembly of Collegiate Schools of Business, 1969.

Calvert, Robert, Jr. Career Patterns of Liberal Arts Graduates. Cranston, R. I.: Carrol Press, 1969.

Clark, John J. Educating Tomorrow's Managers: Business Schools and the Business Community. New York: Committee for Economic Development, 1964.

Clarke, John J., and Blaise J. Opulente. The Impact of the Foundation Reports on Business Education. New York: St. John's University Press, 1963.

Committee for Economic Development. Educating Tomorrow's Managers. New York: Committee for Economic Development, 1964.

Constitution and Standards for Membership. St. Louis: American Association of Collegiate Schools of Business, 1962.

Dale, E. "Social and Moral Responsibilities of the Executive in the Large Corporation." American Economic Review: Papers and Proceedings 51 (May 1961): 540-63.

Federick, W. C. "The Coming Showdown in the Business School." Collegiate News and Views 14, no. 2 (December 1960): 2.

Frank, S., and W. Benton. "Failure of the Business Schools." Saturday Evening Post, February 18, 1961, p. 26.

"Getting More out of the Graduate." Business Week, June 18, 1966, pp. 61-64.

Kniffin, Fred W. "Marketing Education Is Drifting." Journal of Marketing 30 (January 1966): 4-6.

Luck, David J. "Is Marketing Education Driving or Drifting?" Journal of Marketing 28 (April 1965): 22-24.

Neuberger, L. M. "The Everchanging Business Curriculum." Collegiate News and Views, vol. 13 (March 1960).

"New Look in Business Schools." Business Week, June 17, 1961, pp. 157-64.

Nistal, Gerard E. "Career Preparation for Creative and Administrative Positions in Industrial Marketing." Master's thesis, New York University, 1958.

Oliker, L. Richard. "Innovative Approaches to Business Education." Paper presented before the American Assembly of Collegiate Schools of Business, Kansas City, 1972.

Opulente, Blaise J. "Role of the Liberal Arts in a Business Curriculum." In Toward a Philosophy of Business Education, edited by Blaise J. Opulente. Thought Patterns, vol. 8. New York: St. John's University Press, 1960.

Simonds, Rollin H. "Skills Businessmen Use Most." Nation's Business 48 (November 1969): 88.

"Tailoring the B-School to New Business World." Business Week, January 19, 1963, pp. 73-76.

U. S. , Office of Education. Earned Degrees Conferred by Higher Educational Institutions, 1959-1960 (Circular no. 687). Washington, D. C.: Government Printing Office, 1962.

THE PROFESSIONAL SCHOOL ERA:
1970 TO THE PRESENT

Abrego, P. "From Liberal Arts to a Career." Journal of College Placement 38 (Winter 1978): 60-64.

Adams, D. A. "Significant Trends in Professional Development." American Vocational Journal 51 (October 1976): 22-26.

Arbuckle, E. C. "Today's Challenge to Business Education." Business Education Forum 31 (October 1976): 17-19.

Bach, George L. "Whither Education for Business: 1950-2000?" AACSB Bulletin 11 (1975): 13.

Baherman, R. D. "What the Business Community Thinks about Vocational Education." Vocational Education Journal 54 (November-December 1979): 18.

Bahr, G., and R. P. Wegforth. "Historical Development of an Economic Emphasis in Business Education." In National Business Education, edited by Ruth B. Wooschlager and E. Edward Harris. New York: Business Education Association, 1976.

Baily, L. J., and R. W. Stadt. Career Education: New Approaches to Human Development. Bloomington, Ill.: McKnight, 1973.

Balsey, I. W. "Full Service Philosophy of Schools of Business: Discussion." Journal of Business Education 55 (January 1980): 47-48.

Bartholome, L. W. "Back to the Basics in Business Education." Business Education Forum 33 (November 1978): 52-53.

Benson, R. K., and M. A. Parson. "Turning the System Around: Cooperation between Business and College." Community College Review 6 (Winter 1979): 60-64.

Berson, James. "Business Wants the Generalist." Journal of Business Education 50 (March 1975): 50-56.

"The Big Business of Teaching Managers." Business Week, July 25, 1977, pp. 106-8.

Blitstein, Alan. "What Employers Are Seeking in Business Graduates." Collegiate Forum, Winter 1980/81, p. 7.

Boroson, Warren. "The New Careerism on Campus." Money, vol. 5 (April 1976).

Boyer, E. "Academic or Vocational: The False Dichotomy." Vocational Education 54 (March 1979): 18.

"Bridging the Gap between Business and Business Schools." Financial Executive 49, no. 9 (September 1981): 12-15.

Brown, K. W., and M. C. Keap. "Career Education: Golden Opportunity to Revitalize the Business Education Curriculum." Business Education Forum 31 (February 1977): 5-7.

Brown, R. E. "New Age for Education and Business." Change 11 (May-June 1979): 14-16.

Brubacher, John S., and Willis Rudy. Higher Education in Transition. New York: Harper & Row, 1976.

Carlock, L. L. "Accept No Substitute for Excellence." Business Education Forum 34 (December 1979): 16-17.

Carnegie Commission. College Graduates and Jobs. New York: McGraw-Hill, 1973.

_____. Less Time, More Options. New York: McGraw-Hill, 1971.

_____. Priorities for Action. New York: McGraw-Hill, 1973.

Carpenter, D. A. "Bridging the Gap between Vocational Education and the Liberal Arts." Community College Review 6 (Winter 1979): 13-29.

Chasin, J., and G. Benson. "Entry-Level Positions: Do Business Schools Really Give an Advantage?" Journal of College Placement 37 (Fall 1976): 73-77.

Cheit, Earl F. The Useful Arts and the Liberal Tradition. New York: McGraw-Hill, 1975.

Chen, G. K. C., and E. A. Zane. "The Business School Core Curricula Eight Years after Gordon-Howell and Pierson Reports." Collegiate News and Views, vol. 22 (October 1969).

Collins, H. "Corporate Campus: Learning Your Way to a Better Job." Change 11 (July-August 1979): 67-68.

Cooke, L. M. "Why Business Supports Mastery Learning." Education Leader 37 (November 1979): 124-25.

Cooke, M. A. "The New Vocationalism: Challenge to Liberal Learning." Paper prepared for American Council on Education Academic Internship Programs, 1973. Mimeographed.

Davidson, A. C. "Can Liberal Arts and Occupational Education Get Along?" Community College Front 7 (Fall 1978): 4-8.

Davidson, Justin. "How Businessmen Can Help Schools of Business." Nation's Business, October 1975, pp. 73-74.

Deckey, P. A. "Business Education Goes Interdisciplinary at UNL." Journal of Business Education 53 (November 1977): 76-78.

Doll, R. "Education Might Be the Next Victim of a Corporate Takeover." American School Board Journal 166 (March 1979): 44-45.

Donovan, Marguerite E. "Business, Liberal Arts, and the Transfer Student." Journal of Business Education 51 (January 1976): 87-88.

Doyle, Charles A. "Study and Analysis of the Perceptions of Marketing Executives and Graduates of the Value of Undergraduate Marketing Program." Ph.D. dissertation, Temple University, 1974.

Edge, Alfred G., and Ronald Greenwood. "How Managers Rank Knowledge, Skills, and Attributes Possessed by Business Administration Graduates." AACSB Bulletin 11 (October 1974): 30-34.

Enis, Ben, and Sam Smith. "The Marketing Curriculum of the Seventies: Period of Pendulum?" In Marketing: 1776-1976 and Beyond, edited by Kenneth L. Bernhardt, pp. 25-26. Chicago: American Marketing Association, 1976.

Finch, C. R., and N. A. Sheppard. "Career Education Is Not Vocational Education." Journal of Career Education 2 (1975): 37-46.

Frank, A. C., and B. A. Kirk. "Forestry Students Today." Vocational Guidance Quarterly 19 (December 1970): 119-26.

"The Future of Management Education and the Role of the American Assembly of Collegiate Schools of Business: A Report of the AACSB Educational Innovation Committee." St. Louis, Mo., December 5, 1975. Mimeographed.

Future Talk: Education for the '80's. California State University and Colleges System, no. 7. Sacramento: CSUC System, Office of the Chancellor, June 1974.

Galezian, A. K. "Does the Non-Business Major's Background Matter?" Journal of College Placement 39 (Fall 1978): 67-68.

Giusti, Joseph P., and George R. Lovette. "The Business School in Higher Education." Journal of Business Education 46 (January 1971): 42.

Graf, P. "Basic Business: Program of the Future or Things of the Past?" Journal of Business Education 54 (March 1979): 249-51.

Harris, Norman C., and John F. Grede. Career Education in Colleges. San Francisco: Jossey-Bass, 1977.

Hechinger, F. M. "Corporation in the Classroom." Education Digest 44 (December 1978): 52-54.

Hennessey, J. "Examining the Relationship between Corporations and Business Schools." Intellect 105 (November 1976): 132.

Hensley, Gene, and Mark Schulman. Two Studies on the Role of Business and Industry and Participation in Career Education. Washington, D. C.: National Advisory Council for Career Education, 1977.

Hitchcock, J. "The New Vocationalism." Change, April 1973, pp. 46–50.

Hodgkinson, H. L. Institutions in Transition: A Profile of Change in Higher Education. New York: McGraw-Hill, 1971.

Hofstede, G. "Businessmen and Business School Faculty: A Comparison of Value Systems." Journal of Management Studies 15, no. 2 (1978): 77–87.

Huffman, H. "Leading Edges of Business Education Curriculum Development." National Business Education Yearbook 15 (1977): 229–48.

Jackson, J. H. "Some Teacher Concerns about Competency Based Education." Journal of Business Education 55 (December 1979): 104–6.

Jacobs, P. B. "Basic English Is Back to Basics." Journal of Business Education 54 (November 1978): 79–81.

James, Don L., and Ronald L. Decker. "Does Business Student Preparation Satisfy Personnel Officers?" Collegiate News and Views 27 (Spring 1974): 26–29.

Jorgensen, C. E., and B. J. Schmidt. "Current Status of Vocational Business Education Program Evaluation." Business Education Forum 33 (May 1979): 25–28.

Kessler, M. S. "A Curriculum in Business and Public Communication for Humanities Students." ABCA Bulletin 43, no. 1 (March 1980): 6–7.

Krzystofik, A. T., and S. C. Bridgman. "A Need for Closer Integration of Two- and Four-Year Business Programs." Collegiate News and Views 34 (Spring 1981): 1–6.

Lazer, William. "Marketing Education: Commitment for the 1970's." Journal of Marketing 34 (July 1970): 7-11.

Leslie, Larry, and James Morrison. "Social Change and Professional Education in America." Intellect 102 (March 1974): 356-60.

McGrath, E. J. "The Time Bomb of Technocratic Education." Change 6 (September 1974): 24-29.

McGuire, Joseph W. "The Collegiate Business School Today: Whatever Happened to the World We Knew?" Collegiate News and Views 25 (Spring 1972): 1-5.

Magarrell, J. "Academics and Industry Weigh a New Alliance." Chronicle of Higher Education 17 (February 1979): 1-3.

Mahmoud, Shad, and Creighton Frampton. "An Empirical Investigation of the Marketing Curriculum in AACSB Schools." AACSB Bulletin, vol. 31 (February 1975).

Manzer, J. P. "New Directions for Introduction to Business at the Collegiate Level." Journal of Business Education 54 (December 1978): 123-26.

Marshak, Seymour, and John DeGroot. "Marketing Education Ignores the Market for Their Products." Marketing News, March 25, 1977.

Maxwell, S. R. "Corporate Values and the Business School Curriculum." California Management Review, Fall 1975, pp. 72-77.

Mayhew, L. Graduate and Professional Education. New York: McGraw-Hill, 1980.

Mayhew, L. B., and P. J. Ford. Reform in Graduate and Professional Education. San Francisco: Jossey-Bass, 1974.

Mitchell, R. E., and R. D. Hartog. "Two Business Officials Look at the 80's: Interview: R. E. Mitchell and R. Dean Hartog." American Schools and Universities 51 (November-December 1978): 58-60.

Myers, V. J. "Business Educators Wake Up!" Journal of Business Education 53 (December 1977): 103-4.

"The Mystery of the Business Graduate Who Can't Write." Nation's Business, February 1977, pp. 60-62.

Nanassey, L. C. "Issues and Challenges of General Business in the 1980's." Journal of Business Education 54 (November 1978): 94-95.

Nanassey, L. C., ed. Principles and Trends in Business Education. Indianapolis: Bobbs-Merrill, 1977.

Neel, C. W. "Business School Curriculum Design." National Forum 58, no. 3 (Summer 1978): 7-10.

Neely, S. E., and B. F. Schaffer. "Student Evaluations of Business Courses: Some Findings." Journal of Business Education 54 (May 1979): 366-68.

Ness, Frederick W., and Willard Wirtz. "Education and the World of Work." In Will Higher Education Be Ready for the Eighties? Southern Regional Education Board, 1976.

Nistal, Gerald. "Is Higher Education Responsive to the Needs of the Real World?" Collegiate News and Views 33 (Winter 1979): 7-11.

Ozmon, Howard. Dialogue in the Philosophy of Education. Columbus, Ohio: Merrill, 1972.

Parkhurst, P. E. "Academia and Business: Two Research Perspectives." AV Instruction 22 (November 1977): 59.

Parrow, M. "Changing Values: Implications for Major Social Institutions." Current Issues in Higher Education, 1979, pp. 11-16.

Patton, Arch. "The Coming Flood of Young Executives." Harvard Business Review 54 (September 1976): 20-38.

Picker, J. A. "Ibsen and the B-School." Chronicle of Higher Education 15 (September 1977): 32.

"A Plan to Rate B-Schools by Testing Students." Business Week, November 19, 1979, pp. 171-74.

Pledger, Rosemary. "Future Trends in Business Enrollments." Paper presented at Southern Management Association, Atlanta, 1977.

Porter, B. "Evaluation of a Career Development Program in an Undergraduate Business School." Journal of Cooperative Education 46 (May 1978): 60-68.

Price, R. G. "Whose Business Is Business Education?" Journal of Business Education 54 (April 1979): 292-93.

"Realism Comes to the B-School." Business Week, February 2, 1976, pp. 30-31.

Rick, J. H. "Cause of Instructional Change in Business Education." Journal of Business Education 53 (May 1978): 348-51.

Ristau, R. A. "Career Education and Business Education—The Current Scene." Business Education Forum 32 (January 1978): 5-6.

Roark, A. C. "Academic Scientists Eye the Industry Connection." Chronicle of Higher Education 18 (April 1979): 1, 4.

_____. "Proposed National Patent Policy Aims to Bolster Industry-Campus Relations." Chronicle of Higher Education 19 (November 1979): 13-14.

Roth, E. B. "Emergence of Vocational Education." American Education 15 (April 1979): 29-32.

Sagen, H. B. "Careers, Competencies, and Liberal Education." Liberal Education 65 (Summer 1979): 150-66.

_____. "The Professions: A Neglected Model for Undergraduate Education." Liberal Education 59 (December 1973): 507-19.

Schein, E. H. Professional Education: Some New Directions. New York: McGraw-Hill, 1972.

Schramm, K. "Business Education for the Future." International Labor Review 119, no. 1 (January 1980): 115-27.

Shioe, J., and J. F. Rogers. "School-Business Partnership: A Concept Revitalized." Clearing House 52 (February 1979): 286-90.

Solomon, Lewis C. College as a Training Ground for Jobs. New York: Praeger, 1977.

Steiner, George. "Future Curricula in Schools of Management." AACSB Bulletin 13 (October 1976): 7-12.

Stephenson, J. B. "Efficiency and Vocationalism: Renewed Challenge to General Education." Paper prepared for American Council on Education Academic Internship Program, 1973. Mimeographed.

Stewart, J. R. "Business Education in the 80's and Beyond." American Vocational Journal 52 (October 1977): 48-50.

Strier, Franklin. Business vs. Academia: Report on a Survey of Executive and Faculty Attitudes. Dominguez Hills, Calif.: School of Business, California State University, 1979.

Summer, M. "Teaching Reading Skills in Business Classes." Business Education Forum 34 (December 1979): 20-22.

Swan, P. S. "Forecast for the 80's." Journal of College Placement 40 (Winter 1980): 57-60.

Tschirgi, Harvey D. "What Do Recruiters Really Look for in Candidates?" Journal of College Placement, December 1972-January 1973.

Turner, Robert. "Enrollment Prospects for Collegiate Schools of Business." Business Horizons, October 1976, pp. 55-64.

Varner, Iris I. "A Liberal Education Should Include the Study of Business." Chronicle of Higher Education 18 (May 1979): 23.

Vehling, B. S. "Education for Work: Why, What and How." Journal of College Placement 39 (Summer 1979): 24-27.

Wenz, M. F. "Business Education: Is It Being Properly Taught? Is It Realistic?" Journal of Business Education 53 (December 1977): 98-99.

Werner, P. F. "Goal: Career Planning in Basic Business Classes." Business Education Forum 34 (November 1979): 27-29.

West, B. R. "Changing Task of Professional Development: Symposium." American Vocational Journal 51 (December 1976): 24-28.

"What Are They Teaching in the Business Schools?" Business Week, November 10, 1980, pp. 61-69.

Yanter, J. T. "University and Industry as Partners in Education." Phi Delta Kappan 60 (April 1979): 608.

Youngs, B. B., and R. D. Brooks. "Education and Business-Work Relations." College Student Journal 13 (Summer 1979): 206-9.

Zoffer, H. J. "Restructuring Management Education." Management Review 70, no. 4 (April 1981): 37-41.

INDEX

ABOUT THE AUTHOR

PAUL S. HUGSTAD holds the B.A. degree in both English and economics from St. Olaf College. His M.B.A. from the University of Arizona and Ph.D. from the University of Wisconsin are both in business administration. In the past 15 years he has taught at a variety of both private and public institutions in the United States, Canada, and England. Dr. Hugstad has lectured nationally on the relationship of the business school to the liberal arts and the broader university under grants from the Carnegie Foundation, the Shelby Cullom Davis Foundation, and others.

More than a dozen of Dr. Hugstad's more than 50 research publications have dealt specifically with higher education, including articles in education journals such as Liberal Education and Change, in addition to a number of business journals.

Dr. Hugstad's university administration experience has included chairing departmental and school curriculum committees, initially directing the Center for Professional Development at California State University, Fullerton, and membership on the Dean's and Presidential Task Forces on University Goals and Priorities. He was selected by the American Assembly of Collegiate Schools of Business to serve under a national administrative faculty fellowship program in Washington, D.C. (1977-80). Dr. Hugstad has also served as a management consultant to a number of colleges and universities across the country in the area of strategic and marketing planning for education. He is listed in Who's Who in America, Who's Who in the West, and Who's Who in Business and Industry.